THAT WAS MY RAILWAY

THAT WAS MY RAILWAY

From ploughman's kid to railway boss, 1922-1969

by

Frank L. Hick FCIT

Foreword by Sir Robert Reid CBE
Chairman, British Railways Board
1983–1990

Silver Link Publishing Ltd

First published in March 1991

British Library Cataloguing in Publication Data
Hick, Frank L. *1905–*
That was my railway: from ploughman's kid to railway boss
1922–1969.
1. Great Britain. Railways
I. Title
385.092
ISBN 0 947971 56 4

Silver Link Publishing Ltd
The Trundle
Ringstead Road
Great Addington
Kettering
Northamptonshire NN14 4BW

Typeset by The Northampton TypeFoundry, Northampton.
Printed and bound in Great Britain by Mackays of Chatham PLC, Chatham, Kent.

CONTENTS

FOREWORD

by Sir Robert Reid CBE
Chairman, British Railways
Board, 1983–90

Frank Hick's autobiography gives a fascinating picture of a railwayman's life in the North East from 1922 to 1969. I commend it to anyone who has worked for our railway. It will remind them vividly of similar incidents in their own careers. It is also a mine of information for the railway historian and enthusiast.

It describes the wide scope and variety of a railwayman's life, in Frank's case from station clerk to Operating Chief, from Rates Clerk to Signalling Inspector, from Trustee of Convalescent Homes to a Regional Civil Defence Officer. His was the very epitome of a railwayman's life – hard work, long hours, working with marvellous people, the whole pervaded by a strong sense of duty and service to the community. A life of resourcefulness and dedication.

Above all, it demonstrates how it was possible for the son of a Yorkshire hill farmer, with only the most basic education, to rise through the ranks to a very senior post in Regional Headquarters. In the process he became an innovator of change both in organisation and operations, the introduction of diesel railcar operations between Leeds and Bradford in the early 1950s being perhaps the best example.

For anyone with an interest in railways, in the management of a large service industry, or in the minute detail of the everyday life of a railway, this book is a treasure chest of information.

Frank has made a valuable contribution to the history of railways in Great Britain both with this book and his own life's work in the railway.

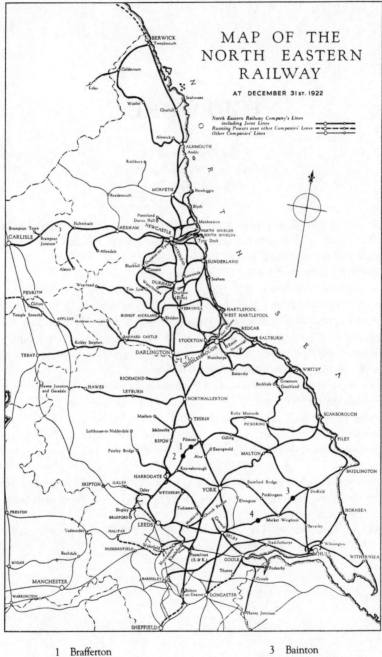

1 Brafferton   3 Bainton
2 Boroughbridge   4 Foggathorpe

The railway I joined in 1922.

INTRODUCTION

For most of my railway life, which started nearly 70 years ago, I worked in close relation to the 'real' things in railway operation, and the following story brings the reader, step by step by actual experience, to the 'sharp end' of running a railway. I have abstained from commenting on locomotive performance or highlighting the romanticism of the steam age, which nevertheless was my 'age'. I realise that other people, better equipped than I, have done that already, though I must say I have been tempted to stray into this attractive field, especially when I recall so vividly my feelings at seeing the first-built brand new Gresley 'A3' 'Pacific' on its debut at York station. To me, a giant – alive – a symbol of my future.

Only sparingly is comment made on the formation, or the pros and cons, of high policy. An operator is essentially a 'doer' within the framework of policy laid down, and if he is to be answerable for results within his function he must have control on a functional basis. How that became a major concern of mine in later years is revealed.

Meanwhile, I have described the journey from farm lad to a probationary clerk at a country station, where an initial set-back was caused by my omitting 'Sir' when addressing the Station Master. Then my experiences at various stations on the hills and in the valleys; my translation to the 'marble halls' of York headquarters and the subsequent struggle to obtain some kind of recognition; the desire to enter the sphere of 'safety' concern through the inspectorate; and later the efforts in the war years to deal with the acute traffic working problems and movement – a historical period in exceptional conditions. Later I moved into senior planning activities following the run-down by war effort, then into the sphere of general management thinking, followed by control of the largest department in the North Eastern Region.

This story is designed to focus on the activities and responsibilities of one man's participation in a major and fascinating industry during a vital time in the country's history. It also, I hope, contains in itself historical interest in presenting a record of former practices at various levels on the railway system of the North East between 1922 and 1969 which, all my life, was 'my railway'.

ACKNOWLEDGEMENTS

I am grateful to Patrick Howat who initiated the idea of recording my railway experience; to the *Yorkshire Evening Press* and *Railnews* for agreeing to the reproduction of extracts from their columns; and to all those who have contributed over the years to my experiences during an interesting and happy career. I also fully acknowledge the source of extracts from *Mile by Mile on the LNER* by S. N. Pike, published by Atlas Publishing and Distributing Co Ltd, whose successors I have been unable to trace.

A portrait of me, 1927-style, drawn by nine-year-old Naomi Stanley, who lives in my village (see page 39).

1.

THE COUNTRY STATION

I was a farmer's boy, and no wonder! My name, 'Hick', according to the Oxford Dictionary, means 'a yokel', and in America, 'a clodhopper'. I was born in 'the horse and cart' era and, coming from that background, when I met a farmer acquaintance as soon as I had joined the railway, he said, 'Thoo's nobbut cum ere as a bloody ink slinger'. Very complimentary! On leaving the railway on retirement, a different acquaintance (of course) said, 'Well, every dog has his day'! That's the world we live in. I went straight off the land into a country railway station office in the year 1922, and retired as a senior railway officer in 1969.

Born in 1905, I received practically no schooling from 11 years of age as I had to help to contribute to my widowed mother's home, and during the First World War exemption from school was allowed and farmers competed for 'child labour', as their men had gone to the war. So I worked on farms with horses, with sheep, with cattle and poultry, and with all the impedimenta of machinery then available. I was in tune with it and loved the closeness to nature, dubbing myself 'ploughman's kid'!

I was born at Harwood Dale, near Scarborough, the fourth child of a hill farmer who died when I was $2^1/2$ years old, leaving my mother with a survival problem. We eventually settled in a charming village in the Vale of York called Myton-on-Swale. By the time I was 15, I started thinking of my future. Could I find a new outlet despite my being 15 miles north of York, isolated in the country, with a bicycle as my only means of transport? A future which would give me a new horizon, wider and more interesting? As it was, I knew I would be confined to being a farm worker as all my acquaintances were, though the sons of farmers in this area had better prospects. I was unqualified in a scholastic sense to claim any grounds for entry into anything but farming and, having pursued no studies in school subjects, I decided to start from scratch by taking up a basic syllabus. Still conscious of the sea from childhood, and perhaps prompted by the fact that the local school-teacher's son was training for the merchant navy, I had an idea of going to sea. He came home with glowing accounts of experiences on his training ship and his prospects for travel. I soon found out, however, that for a career in that direction I must have at least some qualification from, say, a grammar school. Then someone suggested the post office; and a large oil firm delivering paraffin to the area suggested that I join them, but this meant moving to Ripon, away from home. A traveller from Thirsk suggested the railway, where his son was employed. There being a railway station at Brafferton, 3 miles away, I cogitated on this. Railways sounded romantic, more exciting than the post office and more on home ground, so I approached the headquarters of the North Eastern Railway Company at York, requesting details of their requirements for appointment as a junior clerk.

On receipt of this information I realised more fully how inadequate I was. However, one day I had occasion to take a load of grain by horse-drawn wagon to Brafferton station, and, there I spoke to the clerk, who cheered me further by explaining the type of youth required. You must have a good education – a university or public school would exempt you from taking the entrance examination, otherwise you had to sit this test which called for a sound preparation in a number of subjects. He cited the names of two boys he knew who travelled daily to York to a school which specialised in preparing candidates for railway entrance examinations. Also, there was in York, because of its large railway industry, a continuous demand for new entrants with appropriate educational standards.

I understood that there were two regular clerks and a Station Master at Brafferton with an extra clerk in the busy springtime when a firm of seed merchants, T. N. Driffield & Sons, were dispatching their goods. Surely, therefore, there would be a vacancy in due course, and I might stand a chance of perhaps a short-term temporary job. There was little encouragement elsewhere as I made further enquiries, but, nothing daunted, I went to see my former school-teacher and typically she offered her help, and by so doing raised my morale considerably.

She was a good teacher. I got myself the appropriate books, set myself a programme (taking into account that I was on farm work all day) and disciplined myself to concentrate on the subjects in which I had to qualify from 6.00 pm to 9.30 pm every evening except Saturdays and Sundays. These were English (including essay writing), arithmetic, geography, history and general knowledge, to me a formidable list. It was fairly easy to concentrate during the winter months, but in summer it was horrible! Cricket, fishing and other attractions called me, but I stuck to my guns and after a year began to feel reassured as to my ability to tackle the entrance examinations as required.

In response to my request to the North Eastern Railway to sit for this exam, I was invited to attend at York headquarters. I had never seen the inside of an office so large, a completely new experience, and, of course, I had never tackled an examination paper of this calibre. When I saw the set paper my spirits fell, but I remembered the advice of my teacher not to be put off by anything, so I set about trying to answer the questions. Afterwards, overawed, apprehensive, wondering, the country lad made his way back home by train to Brafferton station, then by bicycle. A further morale-boosting session from my mother and teacher, and a renewal of my own determination, brought me back immediately to further study. When I was advised of the results of the examination, I was told that although I had failed on

14

Letters to be addressed.

"THE GENERAL MANAGER,"
Staff Section.
NORTH EASTERN RAILWAY,

YORK.

K.M. 2397.   31st October 1921.

DEAR SIR,

JUNIOR CLERKSHIPS.

REFERRING TO YOUR APPLICATION FOR A JUNIOR CLERKSHIP IN THIS COMPANY'S SERVICE.

I SHALL BE GLAD IF YOU WILL ARRANGE TO ATTEND AT ROOM NO. 104, HEAD OFFICES, YORK, ON Thursday THE 3rd proximo AT 3-0 p.M., FOR THE PURPOSE OF BEING EXAMINED BY THE COMPANY'S MEDICAL INSPECTOR.

I ENCLOSE A PASS FOR YOUR JOURNEY.

Mr F.Hick,
  Myton-on-Swale,
    Helperby.
      Yorks.

YOURS TRULY,

KENELM KERR.

FOR GENERAL MANAGER.

this occasion I had done sufficiently well to take it again. A glimmer of hope!

I enlisted the help of yet another former school-teacher who lived in the next village to mine, cycling to his home some 3 miles each way through all weathers, twice a week. He was particularly helpful with arithmetic, my weakest subject, and was extremely firm with me regarding doing as he instructed and as much as he required. It was good tuition and I appreciated it, remembering his sincere words to me the night before my second examination: 'My boy, this may be the turning point in your life, so do your best'. And I did.

I went off for the further test, but with not quite the same uncertain feelings and, of course, I now knew my way about. I was delighted to meet for the second time others who had evidently faired the same as me, and also saw the two youths to whom the station clerk had referred. This time I coped better. I had more confidence. The way home was brighter! So imagine the delight when I received a letter asking me to report for a medical test. That meant one thing – I had satisfied the examiners on the written test. It also meant that I had to pass a medical and eyesight examination, including colour vision. Having in due course successfully passed these, I then had an oral test and interview in the District Goods Manager's office in Leeds where I was told I must qualify in shorthand and typewriting within 12 months, something every new entrant at this level had to do. These subjects were foreign to me, and furthermore the nearest tuition centre was York, quite impossible for me to attend on a regular basis .

I waited months for a letter of appointment which I had been promised, and it was a trying time. Nobody outside my immediate family circle believed I had succeeded, and even my employers on the farm stopped looking for a successor! I had to keep milking the cow I looked after, grooming the riding horse belonging to the boss, taking care of the poultry, and so on.

However, the letter, dated 25 April 1922, eventually came, appointing me as from 1 May to the place I wanted to reach, Brafferton station, and I suddenly had a new zest for life. I had visions of more amenable working conditions, of holidays (something I had never had), better working hours, better dress, status, new experience – so very much to look forward to. I worked out my 'notice' on the farm – mowed nettles with that old scythe, but now slashed at them with great vigour, the animals got extra rations, and the boss's shoes never shone so brightly. It was good to show my employer that I had proved I could make it against his, and his autocratic mother's, prediction that 'I hadn't a chance'.

So, on Monday 1 May 1922 I got on my bike (literally) and cycled to Brafferton station to join North Eastern Railway (the NER, initials which were immediately meaningful to me, remained so all my railway life, and still are). It was the home of the cradle of railways, its boundaries stretching from Berwick in the north to Shaftholme Junction (just north of Doncaster) in the south, and from the North Sea in the east to the Pennines and the Wharfe in the west, and was soon to become part of the amalgamated group, LNER (London & North Eastern Railway).

Letters to be addressed.

"THE GENERAL MANAGER,"
Staff Section.
NORTH EASTERN RAILWAY,

YORK.

K.M.2397.   4th November 1921.

Dear Sir,

JUNIOR CLERKSHIPS

I have to inform you that the reports of your examination are satisfactory and your name has been entered on the list of passed candidates for appointment.

Yours truly,

KENELM KERR. S.

for General Manager.

Mr F.Hick,
   Myton-on-Swale.
      Helperby.
         Yorks.

A. BROWN. J.SHAW.
DISTRICT GOODS MANAGER.

Telegraphic Address:
"Brown Goods Northeastern Leeds"
Telephone No. 20336.

GS. 9775.

Letters to be addressed:

"DISTRICT GOODS MANAGER,"

NORTH EASTERN RAILWAY,

April 21st. 1922.   LEEDS.

Mr. F. Hick,
   Myton-on-Swale,
     Helperby,
       Yorks.

Dear Sir,

Your application for Junior Clerkship has been passed on to me, and I should like you to come over and see me at my Office in Wellington Street on Tuesday morning next, April 25th. I enclose a pass which will enable you to travel free of charge from Brafferton to Leeds and back.

Yours faithfully,

J. SHAW.

```
A. BROWN.  J. S.IAT.                    Letters to be addressed:
DISTRICT GOODS MANAGER,
                                            "DISTRICT GOODS MANAGER,"
   Telegraphic Address:
"Brown Goods Northeastern Leeds"            NORTH EASTERN RAILWAY,
   Telephone No. 20336.
                                                                LEEDS.
   GS. 9775.                             April 25th. 1922.


   Mr. F. Hick,
        Myton- on- Swale,
            Helperby,
                 Yorks.

   Dear Sir,
                   Referring to your visit to this Office
   today.    I have decided to place you for the present
   at Brafferton station for training, and I shall be glad if
   you will arrange to commence there on Monday next, May 1st.


                   Yours faithfully,

                   J. S.IA".
```

The chief officers in the North Eastern Railway on my appointment were:

General Manager
   Ralph (soon to be Sir Ralph) Wedgwood CBE CMG, who had succeeded
   Sir A. K. Butterworth as from 1 January 1922
Assistant General Manager
   R. Bell CBE
Chief Goods Manager
   Alex Wilson OBE
Passenger Manager
   Kenelm Kerr
General Superintendent
   H. A. Watson
Chief Mechanical Engineer
   Sir Vincent L. Raven

These names meant very little to me until I began to see them on various printed documents from time to time, though the high decorations were certainly impressive.

Of immediate importance was the name of the Station Master at Brafferton, of which I was already aware. I entered the station office very nervously, said 'Good morning' to him and immediately got into trouble for not adding 'Sir' after the greeting. I had learned my first lesson, and had launched my career!

The Station Master's name was Nathan Raw. He had been at Brafferton since 1901 and was to remain there until 1929 when he retired at the age of 64. He was austere and educated, quite an outstanding man in his environment. Station Masters at country stations were important people in the village hierarchy, the ranking of which was in the order of (1) squire, (2) parson and (3) Station Master, especially so at the time I walked into that office. He was in a position to provide vital facilities to many people, especially the farmers using the railway. He was a real old-fashioned disciplinarian who expected everything to be done right and to schedule. He smoked a pipe, 'puffing and blowing' when dealing with a contentious matter, and half ran, half walked, when going from one job to another. He also had a reputation of being tight-fisted, the name 'Nathan' being used by some locals in a derogatory way. He was, in short, a big man in a small place.

He lived in the station house, as was the normal practice in the service. His working day started just after 8 in the morning, unless for any reason he had to take the early turn in the booking office. On taking up duty he would look round the office and, having established from the clerk on duty that all was well, would visit the signal box and the station generally. He would review the arrangements for the day, especially the wagon requirements for forwarding traffic, and deal with any coal orders, especially those for which he had delivery arrangements to initiate.

Brafferton station itself was set at the northern end of a deep cutting just outside the combined villages of Brafferton and Helperby. It had one platform, although there were strong signs that there had once been a second track. The station house was a big four-square building, solid and impressive, and it appeared that from the upstairs windows especially there would be splendid views of the Hambleton Hills and North Yorkshire Moors, the White Horse being a prominent feature of the view.

In addition to the Station Master, there were two permanent clerks at Brafferton; one was Percy Wharton, who later left the railway, and the other was Charlie Sellars, who eventually became Station Master at Poole-in-Wharfedale. There was also a temporary clerk during the time that goods traffic was at its seasonal peak, but when the seed time thinned out this temporary appointee was transferred to some other station. There were two porter-signalmen, Walter Nicholls (who, when asked what he liked better than a pint of beer, said 'Two') and Charlie Ford – excellent chaps – who worked between them the full day, doing the signalling and station work and the portering in both passenger and freight spheres. Train signalling was by the 'staff and ticket' system for single line working, with conventional semaphore signals. The 'block posts' on either side were Boroughbridge to the west and Pilmoor to the east.

One feature of the station office which first intrigued me was the almost constant tick-tack of the single needle telegraph instrument, the means of railway communication beyond the next station. A system used throughout the railway, and I believe peculiar to railways, it was a Morse code device. Messages from and to Brafferton were interpreted by this means and as it was a general circuit with a number of station codes included, we were identified by our own code. Our code was BF, and York telegraph office, the central point for transmission of all messages outside the circuit, was YK, and I had to learn how to operate it otherwise when I was alone at the station Brafferton would be isolated. The first message I sent was the daily wagon report, which, with its wagon codes, was a good testing effort, but it took me a long time to be able to receive satisfactorily. I never reached the stage that my experienced colleagues had attained, of being able to hold a conversation at the same time as receiving or sending a message. These instruments I later found were often in signal boxes, where the men were experts.

On joining the staff I had to work shifts, and when on early turn I started in time to receive the first train from Harrogate to Pilmoor at 7.00 am. This train collected passengers for Pilmoor, there to change for York and the south, or the north. One or two people travelled daily to their work at Thirsk, but the majority were for York, as it was quicker to travel to York that way than the alternative via Knaresborough. This early morning train was lightly loaded, but in any case had to go to Pilmoor to enable the engine to run round its train for the return working.

Its return journey was better supported by people working in Knaresborough or Harrogate. There were also schoolchildren for Knaresborough Grammar School and for Harrogate College. To complete the service, there was a mid-day train up and down, then one again in the evening. There was also a late train on Saturday evening; I used to go into Harrogate myself on Saturday afternoons when I was off duty, returning by this service. There were three coaches on it, composed of compartmented stock, including three 1st class compartments.

Within two months of starting at Brafferton I found myself on duty on my own. I had to sell tickets, book parcels and authorise the guard to set the train away. I also had to cash up each evening, and lock up the money in a safe place ready for the morning clerk to place the cash bag in a travelling 'safe' conveyed in the guard's van of the first train next day. This was the universal method of transferring each station's cash takings to a central point at York; a balance sheet accompanied the leather bag, duly locked up, and it was acknowledged by the cashier who received it by rail post.

It gave me a great sense of importance to have to make sure that all carriage doors on departing trains were properly closed, and then give the hand signal to the guard to start the train. Here was I, a 17-year-old lad, in charge of railway working after only a couple of months on the job, giving this 'right away' signal to the guard for real live trains to start. A great sense of accomplishment, and an exciting way of starting a railway career!

I soon had to begin to think of other things beyond the confines of Brafferton station. As I have said, probationary clerks had to pass an examination in shorthand and typing within a year of joining the service, and I had no experience in either, nor were there any people in the locality to teach me those two subjects – a serious problem began to loom ahead. I therefore had to think how and where I could get tuition. In addition, I had to satisfy the powers that be that I could do the elementary station accounts and be generally acceptable to the Station Masters reporting on me. I therefore concentrated on this latter item first.

The pattern of passenger traffic was mainly from village to town, (predominantly York, Harrogate and Knaresborough) and return, with extra traffic on market days, an attraction to people producing farm and similar produce. So often on those days passengers would turn up as the train was approaching the station, causing minor panic in the office since they all had to be issued with tickets and excess charges for exceptional bulk produce. The small cardboard tickets held alphabetically in a rack near the issuing window were dated on the back when issued by plunging them into a machine. This became a familiar sound.

Concerning the traffic in the reverse direction, I remember particularly a regular passenger to the station who was a Prudential Insurance man, surely a national figure in those early days of life insurance. Nearly all the families in the villages were persuaded to pay a penny or twopence a week for insurance, mostly 'on death' to pay for their funeral! The 'Man from the Pru' (early version, or was he the original?) came from Harrogate at regular intervals to collect these premiums. He would get off the early train with his bicycle and would visit the villages of Brafferton, Helperby, Myton, Tholthorpe, Cundall and, no doubt, a wide radius around the central point of the station. In the evening he would catch the 6 o'clock train back to Harrogate. As he sat in the waiting room, lit, like all the rooms throughout the station, by oil lights, waiting for the train back home, I would hear him setting out his cash on the wooden seats, counting out his takings for the day. I remember his name – it was Botteril – and it suited him. A tall, slim figure, dressed in a dark suit, pale complexion, with a wide brimmed black hat, he was a character straight out of *Don Quixote*. He also had the best bike, one with a chain case, that I had ever seen.

In the summer we used to run excursions from Brafferton, which we might arrange jointly with Boroughbridge or some other station, to Scarborough. Sometimes the trains went via York and sometimes via Gilling and Malton. There would be three or four during the summer, taking all the kids to the seaside and back – I don't remember them going anywhere else but Scarborough in those days. They were certainly 'high days' in the locality.

Brafferton was a comparatively small station and when I went there on 1 May it was a busy time. Near to the station was a firm of seed merchants, T. N. Driffield & Sons, and at that period of the year the three clerks were kept busy dealing with the seasonal traffic. Some seed parcels were sent by passenger train, at the higher rate applicable to traffic sent by that means and some were sent by what was then known as the road wagon service on the freight train at freight train rates. The seeds were packed in strong white jute bags weighing from a pound or two to one hundredweight or more. There were three or four deliveries from the seed farm each day at the height of the season.

Everything going by freight train had to be individually invoiced, while for that travelling by passenger train the label had to be stamped with the appropriate value of parcels stamps and recorded in the dispatch book. The distribution was nationwide so our geography was tested every day.

Like many Station Masters in those days, Mr Raw had a coal sale, and this was an important aspect of his work. He also had a financial interest in it, and looked after it personally, so far as he could. The coal sale arrangement was instituted by the

NER, which was I believe the only railway which encouraged this form of business.

At large stations such as York, or even medium-sized places, there was an appointment separate from the Station Master known as depot agent, and I recall that people with quite senior jobs (to my way of thinking then!) in headquarters elected to take up a station coal agency because the personal annual income was higher by doing so, and with less responsibility! Some Station Masters, once they had developed a substantial coal sale decided to stay where they were and not apply for promotion. Places such as Bedale or Church Fenton brought in a higher income for the Station Master than that earned by the local District Officer!

The station staff were required to perform the weighing of the coal – the empty cart in, the loaded cart out – for which every coal sale station was provided with a large vehicle weighing machine. We also had to issue the appropriate document, and collect the money on cash transactions. Anyone taking delivery of coal not processed through the Station Master had to pay weighing charges.

Separate records were kept for the coal business, and usually the Station Master reserved for himself the keeping of coal accounts. There was a close relationship between collieries and the Station Master, since he could influence the type of coal sold. Colliery representatives used to visit stations frequently, and I think some of them were provided with travel passes. The quick release of the privately-owned wagons was of importance to coal factors (as it was also for the railway's own common-user wagons) and this was facilitated by many stations being provided with strongly-built coal cells with the rail lines above at a higher level and capable of bearing the weight of loaded wagons and locomotive. Each cell was labelled with the name and type of coal, ie the colliery from which the coal was received (such as Whitwood), so that customers could select their favourite fuel, some house coal being distinctly better, but dearer, than others. The incoming wagons were placed over the appropriate cell by the branch line goods train, and the contents were then discharged by releasing the bottom doors of the wagons. Where cells were not provided, as at later stations at which I served, the coal had to be shovelled out of side-door wagons, a laborious procedure. As almost everybody in the locality depended on coal for heating and cooking, there was a constant flow of trade in horse-and-cart deliveries.

The goods train which served the branch was based at Starbeck, near Harrogate, which was a concentration point for freight traffic over a wide area. This is where the 'pick-up' services (the common name for a branch line goods train) were made up from incoming trains from Leeds and York to service the local branches such as ours, or those to Pateley Bridge, Wetherby, Leeds Northern and Harrogate itself. It was also where locomotives suitable for branch line working were housed and serviced, and where 'smalls' (less than wagon-load goods) were transhipped, sorted and distributed, this being typical of freight organisation throughout the country.

When our train was made up there in the early hours of each weekday, it was programmed to cover the stations of Copgrove, Boroughbridge (where there were two sidings away from the main station to work, at Roecliffe, which catered for a busy brickyard, and Humberton, a farming loading and unloading point), Brafferton and Pilmoor. Boroughbridge was by far the busiest station on the branch. At each station the train had to place wagons in position according to requirements – coal wagons over the cells for bottom door discharge by gravity, perhaps livestock from Ireland to be placed at a suitable off-loading dock, or a wheeled machine on a 'flat' wagon requiring an end dock, and so on. Every day that train was awaited by someone expecting a particular consignment, like people wait for the morning postman – often a farmer would be waiting for either an urgent load of livestock or an empty wagon for loading.

The various track layouts could result in some train movements being difficult to make in order to place wagons in the desired position. To help deal with this was a practice known as 'fly-shunting'. This movement was officially frowned upon, but everyone directing the operation did it. At Brafferton, 'fly-shunting' was used to get a wagon off the down goods train on to the coal cell siding. The wagon had to be transferred from the rear of the engine to the front, so that it could then be propelled to the required position. As there was no 'run round' facility, the method of doing this was for the engine, with only the wagon in question attached, to proceed along the main line from the Boroughbridge direction until it was going at a fairly good speed and approaching the station yard turn-off points. The guard would run alongside to control the wagon and, at the right moment, would release the coupling between the wagon and the engine without too radically affecting its speed. The engine would then accelerate away and the signalman would change the points immediately that it was clear of them. The wagon, now with enough momentum, would enter the siding and run up the gradient on to the coal depot. The signalman had to time the points change accurately, but the sheer delicacy of the operation prompted the right kind of care which guaranteed its success! The guards became adept at the move, and any shortfall in the required length of the wagon's journey was supplemented by the use of a heavy, long cast iron pinch-bar by which one could inch wagons forward.

The alternative way of making the transfer of a wagon from the rear of the engine to the front was to place the wagon on a siding parallel with another on which the engine could stand. A hauling rope was then attached from locomotive to wagon, and the latter was hauled beyond a pair of points. Disconnect the rope, change the points, and the engine could then place the wagon in position. It was a longer process, but preferred by some.

Grain and potatoes were the main bulk traffics at Brafferton. All the grain, a very important commodity from the surrounding farms, was conveyed in railway sacks which were hired out and were an essential item both to the farmer and the railway. The railway sack would hold 12 stones of oats, 16 stones of barley and 18 stones of wheat and rye. The farm men, in transferring grain from farm wagon to rail wagon, often had to carry these weights on their backs, or otherwise man-handle them inch by inch.

Railway sacks were a separate trading item and they had an independent value which they carried with them wherever they were. They had to be carefully accounted for and at the end of each month a 'balance' was compiled. This balance at a busy station was invariably a tricky manoeuvre and on occasions needed some imagination! Station clerks detested this item at the end of the month, since there were so many directions in which sacks could be lost, wrongly declared or otherwise misrepresented. Some 'grain' stations dealt with thousands a month. The jute sacks were made to a high standard, and could withstand, as they often had to, rough handling. Any damage by wet or vermin meant the sack(s) being sent to the central supply depot in York where a squad of women were employed in repair work. In fact, I was given to understand that over 5 million sacks were in railway stock and, as someone put it, the stock of BR sacks would have formed a carpet roughly $3^1/2$ yards wide stretching from Land's End to John O'Groats.

Potatoes also were transported by rail in sacks, but these were provided by the potato merchants and, when full, weighed 8 stones. The empty sacks came in bundles by rail from traders whose name usually appeared on the sacks, and a record was made of them on their way to the farms, as an indication that a consignment of potatoes would soon be on offer. This in turn indicated that a wagon order would be forthcoming, and we had to take account of this in planning future requirements.

In 1922 we were still living with the aftermath of the First World War and the acute run-down of railway equipment. There was a critical wagon shortage and farmers could not just order a wagon and get it on the day requested. They had to plan well in advance and place a firm order to enable us at the station to indent in our daily wagon order to our local supply centre, Starbeck, with no certainty that it would be supplied. The farmers' need for wagons was a national problem and one which they and the station had to scheme and struggle to overcome. In fact, it became a daily problem in the main season of grain and potato loadings, involving many aspects of commercial diplomacy, or perhaps less attractive peculiarities of human behaviour! In short, the clerk on duty at any given time was an influential cog in a very sensitive machine when a farmer's plan stood in jeopardy. The 'farm lad', to his former boss, had changed his spots.

At Brafferton we dealt with quite a variety, and changing patterns, of goods, but we had a regular outward milk traffic in 10-12 gallon churns, and fish in boxes as inward traffic. To see the farmers and porters turning the milk churns on their base rims with one hand, full or empty, along the platform was entertaining, and inevitably some showing off took place. It was a slick achievement. Handling the fish-boxes, with ice melting and fluid running out on to the floor of the guard's van or across the waiting room floor, was another matter. The smell was most offensive, but the fish and chip shops in the area had to be served, and rail service, especially to branch line stations, was the only method of distribution of fish from Hull, Scarborough and other fishing ports. There was one customer who had a flat trap hauled by a fine little pony who hawked fish round the village each day, and he was noted for his clarion call of "errin', fresh 'errin", a plentiful supply always being available. Needless to say, there was always a cleaning up job to do after the fish had been collected.

During the game season we had quite a traffic from the local estates. Colonel Collins of Cundall Manor sent to London each week a consignment of game along with other country items such as butter, eggs, rabbits and poultry in specially prepared hampers. Sir Clive Coates of Helperby Hall and Colonel Stapylton of Myton Hall both used the railway in this way.

As life at the station began to take on a regular rhythm for me, it became a red letter day when the auditors came to check the books. Arriving on the early morning train, they would walk straight to the office. Usually there were two men, the auditor and his assistant. 'Give me the keys,' was the first thing the auditor said, so of course my keys were handed over and access given to the cash drawer, ticket rack, parcel stamps and all cash books, and due obedience shown to all his demands, wondering what the hell he would find! We had no prior knowledge of his proposed visit, of course, and gave a sigh of relief when he had checked the till and found it correct! His return train to Harrogate couldn't come early enough. In lighter vein, I would sometimes see an auditor getting off the early morning train and think 'Oh God, here he is again', and would then see that he had a gun under his arm, so he was evidently joining a shooting party. That was the only time it was pleasant to see an auditor! Of course the railway line itself offered a considerable shooting area, complemented by a lot of woodland and game breeding land adjacent. The embankments were riddled with rabbit warrens, so inevitably the 'auditor' would return with a good bag, very pleased with himself.

The Station Master at Pilmoor had a half-day off each week when normally he and his wife went to York, and it was the practice for a clerk from Brafferton to go to Pilmoor to look after the station in his absence; I took a turn at doing this. The Station Master, Mr Mowforth, a very understanding man who later became SM at Hemingborough, accepted this youthful junior with tolerance and showed me the ropes. To be trusted to perform the job encouraged me no end – in fact, you could say I was 'cock-a-hoop'! I only relieved him of his office duties, the station having only a small clientele of rail passengers; but in order to cater for people changing at Pilmoor, being the junction for the Brafferton and Gilling branches, he ran a side-line selling chocolates, cigarettes, fruit and other sweets for the benefit of the passengers awaiting connections, so I also had this to look after.

Much more to my satisfaction, I took advantage of going into the signal boxes, there being three important boxes under the Pilmoor SM, Pilmoor station, Sessay Wood (the junction box for the Gilling branch) and Sunbeck, a minor box at the apex of the triangle of lines facing the York and North directions a little way up the Gilling line. I also took advantage of learning all I could about Hall's automatic signalling which applied between Alne and Thirsk, the only type of its kind in the country. I also learned a good deal about the main line passenger and freight services, a mysterious world quite beyond my comprehension. There were few main line trains which stopped at Pilmoor during the period and, as I have said before, it did seem quite a responsibility to 'set off' these giant trains, as they appeared to me, a youth of 17 years! It was nevertheless a wonderful experience.

Pilmoor was essentially an 'operating' station, with little commercial interest, placed in a rural area where the main inhabitants were railway people. It had one distinguishing feature – what was known as the 'Signal Sighting' location, where the train-working staff such as drivers, firemen, guards and others concerned with reading semaphore signals were taken to test physically their eyesight over various distances. Little did I think that I would later visit this place in charge of the Signal Sighting Committee in a special saloon train. Those highly-placed semaphore arms, a relic of the past, remained in position for many years, a landmark of the area.

Pilmoor, along with many other stations in the area, was a well-known station for releasing racing pigeons, sent there on the train by fanciers mainly from the northern counties, Northumberland and Durham. About 12 or so birds in each specially constructed basket, they would be dispatched on good flying days by passenger train labelled to the destination station, with a request to the staff to fill in details of release on the tag attached to each hamper, recording the state of weather, the time released, and any special note for the senders' information. The weather conditions had to be favourable for flying and the air space clear of wires and trees. Pilmoor had both these, and many baskets were received daily during the training and racing periods. On a number of occasions I had the experience of acting as 'starter', and it was a great thrill to release large numbers of birds in an excited flutter, to see them circle around, and then, with unerring instinct, make for home.

In the high season, special trains of baskets of pigeons were provided for large racing events, sometimes involving transits to the continent, when birds were accompanied by 'convoyers', men who attended to the needs of the pigeons *en route*. A world of its own!

I was at Brafferton for only a short time, from May to September 1922. In October, November and December I was required to take up duty at York Goods Station. So, a country lad of 17 years, I nervously walked through the Leeman Road tunnel from York Station to take up a probationer clerk's position in the railway goods agent's office. This was a strange and not very happy environmental experience for me, having been born and bred in rural surroundings. I passed beyond the tunnel and was confronted with a large warehouse with office attached.* York Goods Station dealt with railway goods traffic to and from York and a wide area around, for which in those days there was no alternative form of transport. In the sidings of the adjacent yard, traffic in full wagon loads was dealt with, while in the huge warehouse less-than-wagon loads, incoming and/or outgoing, plus transfer traffic, was handled.

I ventured up the steps leading to a wide doorway, through which I passed to a corridor and found my way upstairs. I duly reported to the appropriate person and was directed to take duty in the 'inwards' office. In this large complex there was an 'inwards' office to the left of the entrance hall, and an 'outwards' office to the right, on the ground floor, and an accountancy room and the goods agent's office upstairs. In each office there was a raised dais on which was majestically seated the Chief Clerk of that department. Both men were 'larger than life' – Mr Moll, with his

*In 1990, this building, as the Peter Allen Building, housed the 'Great Railway Show' during the re-roofing of the adjacent National Railway Museum.

fierce moustache and ruddy complexion, presided over the 'inwards' while 'Baggy' Freeman, in liberal tweeds and more like a university professor in sporting outfit than a railway clerk, oversaw the 'outwards'. There they sat, like gods, Moll looking down on clerks who were filling in delivery sheets for draymen, checking on the distribution arrangements, advising consignees of traffic on hand not to be delivered by dray, and so on, while Freeman, from similar dizzy heights, supervised his staff who were charging and invoicing forwarded goods and those connecting with incoming cartage drays.

Joining the 'inwards' office, I soon experienced the activities which gave this building its life and character. There was the constant stream of rail goods wagons moving into and out of the 'loading' bays, the checkers supervising the loading and unloading of each wagon as performed by goods porters, who physically carried packages in their arms, or wheeled them on sack barrows to town delivery drays, to storage points, or to forward service wagons. There was the continuous rattle of sack barrow wheels over the wooden platforms, the voices of men carried above the din and the shunting noises of the local 'pilot' engine sorting the wagons. All this, coupled with the horse-dray activities which dominated one side of the complex, the pungent and offensive smell emanating from every conceivable kind of traffic (vegetables, groceries, etc), the clouds of smoke from the engine sheds opposite (now the National Railway Museum), station and yard locomotives, portrayed to me, one used to open countryside, an undesirable environment and a repudiation of 'England's green and pleasant land'!

I worked there for three months, then requested a transfer. At least I had learned what a checker was, the meaning of 'cartage', and the separate business of horse transport and horse values in a different world from that in which I had previously been associated with horses.

Responding to my request, they moved me to Bainton, a small station on the Yorkshire Wolds. I went there on 1 January 1923, the first day of the railway amalgamation, when the North Eastern Railway became a division of the London & North Eastern Railway.

2.

NEW STATION, NEW COMPANY

I was too young at the time to understand the full significance of the 'grouping', but I know that many of the staff, especially the senior staff, did not like it one little bit. They had a great loyalty and affection for what they considered was 'their' railway. They considered it a 'great' railway as I believe the staff of each constituent of the new groups did of their railway, even though it was not literally prefixed with the word 'Great', as in Great Western, Great Northern, Great Central or Great Eastern. In any event, the initials were now no longer NER but L&NER.

I recall the words of Sir Ralph Wedgwood, who became the first General Manager of the LNER, when he expressed his feelings about the company. He said:

> 'The Old North Eastern Railway lived and throve for nearly 70 years. When it took on a new and less individual life in 1923 it may be doubted if any of those who served it were disposed to welcome the change. New and wider loyalties could only come with the years, and the romance of provincial patriotism dies hard, if indeed it ever passes away.
>
> 'Those who served the North Eastern are proud of their luck. They will read of the steady development of the old undertaking to become the largest dock owner in Great Britain, and (strange to say) the not unpopular monopolist of rail transport in the three northern counties. They will remind themselves that their railway was the first to recognise the Railwaymen's Trade Unions and to settle questions of hours and wages in friendly discussion across the Board Room table, as it was also the first to draw valuable lessons from a study of American railway methods.
>
> 'The North Eastern never lacked leadership, nor did it allow the choice to be limited to its own boundaries; but it looked across the Tweed rather than across the Humber, and the names of Gibb and Geddes testify to the stimulus we received from our northern neighbours. Yet from the Board downwards to the youngest of the rank

and file it was the progressive North-country outlook and the tough
corporate spirit animating the organisation which make its achievement
specially worthy to be kept in remembrance.'

Arriving at Bainton I well remember getting off the train on my first day; cold,
sleeting and inhospitable, as only it can be on that wide open, bleak wold. The
Station Master gave me one glance and said, 'Have they sent me another bloody
kid?' There was no reply to that! I just walked into the office and took stock of the
place, while he went on, 'Can you do monthly accounts?', kicking the bottom
drawer of a desk.

I replied, 'I have had very little experience in that direction but I will have a go.'
'You have no option. Start now!'

His name was Welburn. He had been a signalman, so had little clerical training,
and with a typical broad Yorkshire approach and more than a little vernacular, he
baptised me in the work of his version of station accounts.

It was while I was at Bainton that I had to pass an examination in general
knowledge of station work and also the shorthand and typing test at the end of my
probationary year. Fortunately, the Rector of Bainton parish, a Canon of York
Minster, wrote religious books and had a secretary to help him. This secretary, an
elderly lady, was marvellous to me when she heard of my predicament of having no
one to help in my shorthand and typing. She dictated to me to practise my Pitman's
(which eventually developed into 'Hick's' shorthand) and disciplined my typing,
voluntarily, in her spare time. I was lucky to have such help and I passed the test –
with great relief! Meanwhile, the Station Master had, unknown to me,
recommended that I be appointed to the permanent staff whether I passed the tests
or not! Evidently I had made the grade in his judgement! What was more important
was that on my elevation my wage went up from 19s 11d (I was paying £1 for digs)
to £1 10s per week as from my 18th birthday. From 1d per week in the red I was
now 10s in the black!

At Bainton there was a lot of grain traffic loaded on to rail and this was brought
into the station on 'pole' wagons. This type of farm wagon had a single central shaft
and the two horses hauling the load were harnessed side by side to the wagon itself
by steel link traces on which the stress of pulling the load rested. Although the
horses were attached to the 'pole' by harnesses, the pole itself was more to keep the
horses together and act as the pivot for steering.

Bainton station was located on high ground on the rolling wolds and it was a
delight to stand on the platform and watch the spectacle of a convoy of five or six
pole wagons approaching in the distance, stirring up the dust of the local rough
stone roads, the horses snorting and straining at the traces, hauling their heavy
loads. Entering the station yard, the wagoners manoeuvring the horses so skilfully
into position, shouting their 'arves' and 'gees' with a splash of exhibitionism; it was
quite dramatic and thrilling to a stranger from the flat lands. This form of transport
was in my short experience peculiar to the wolds.

Rail wagons had to be pre-arranged and available to carry these substantial onslaughts at a small station such as Bainton, and the men from the farms found it hard work loading the heavy sacks of grain without mechanical help. All had to be duly checked by the station porters for the purpose of charging, including the recording of the number of railway sacks involved. One could almost imagine the sounding of 'The Retreat' once the mission was completed and the activity died down, the weary horses and men setting out for home. An anticlimax!

This was my first spell away from home, so my 'digs' were most important to me. A middle-aged spinster, of kindly disposition and living with her father, provided the sort of food a young lad liked and plenty of it in real country style. Hers was the recognised railway clerks' home at Bainton. The bearded old man, having spent his earlier life on fishing boats based on Bridlington, had decided to leave the sea and beccome a shepherd controlling a large flock of sheep nearby. Complete with his crook he was the epitome of a wold shepherd – a grand old man. He was also drummer in the Bainton brass band, and so proud of his place at Sunday morning practices. His huge drum hung in his bedroom – it was his pride and joy, the symbol of his achievement. Now and again during the night the drum would crack loudly, as if exploding, due to variations in the temperature, and disturb the whole household!

I was allowed to go home every other weekend when on early turn Saturday. I returned for late turn Monday, there being no Sunday service. I was anxious to see my home and relate to my mother the happenings of the two weeks away. Naturally she was concerned to know about my 'digs' and the conditions of my job, and I was able to reassure her. I myself loved the open wold country, the sweeping landscape of fields of grain and meadow and the rural though different setting of village life. During my weekends on duty I made friends with a farming family, this friendship lasting many years, while my main chum was the son of the local blacksmith who wanted to join the railway through the same channels as I had. I was able to help him in a small way, and he passed the written exam. Tragically, the day he was advised that he could not be accepted because he was colour blind, his father died suddenly of a heart attack, so there was great trouble to contend with in the family which naturally spread to their friends.

Some Sunday evenings were most enjoyable, spent at the Station Master's house. He used to scrape a tune on his violin and together with his grown-up daughter, who was a most accomplished pianist, we would sing favourite songs and hymns. I had been a choirboy from my earliest days so 'a good time was had by all'!

It was at Bainton that I was taught a severe lesson in the need for care when directing passengers. Every Thursday many passengers went to Driffield market, returning in the evening when, in winter, it was dark. On alighting from the train, these people had to cross the running lines at rail level from the arrival platform to reach the station exit. On one occasion, with the incoming locomotive stationary and issuing steam, waiting for the train to arrive from the opposite direction (Bainton was a passing place on an otherwise single line), the passengers hurriedly made for the other side of the line. I failed to control them properly, being busy collecting tickets and not realising what was happening, and before they had reached the point of exit the express coming from the Selby direction thundered menacingly, headlights glaring, towards them. They had the presence of mind to scurry off the track and crouch against the wall of the nearby signal cabin just in time. No one was hurt, but they were terrified and so was I. Luckily there was no backwash, but in future I made doubly sure all was right.

Usually, as I found out later, single lines worked by the 'token' system were branch lines where trains stopped at every block post. Not so at Bainton, where a tablet token was in use which catered for express trains between Bridlington and Leeds. These trains called at Driffield, Market Weighton and Selby only, conveying in a morning a 'club' saloon coach for business commuters, the same vehicles making up the return train in the evening. It was this evening train which came through non-stop on this occasion.

With non-stop trains, a special procedure for exchanging tokens applied. The porter signalman, having collected the token from the train from Driffield, had to put it through the token machine with the co-operation of the signal box at Southburn, and extract a tablet for the incoming express. The signals forward were not to be cleared until he was in possession of this token. The porter signalman would then stand on the platform under the station lamp facing the oncoming train, holding the pouch containing the tablet in his right hand with the token loop across his body at head level leaning somewhat towards the train. His left arm was outstretched at shoulder level to receive from the fireman the incoming token. The fireman, leaning from the cab of the locomotive, would use his arms to make a snatch, simultaneously delivering and receiving, and the train would accelerate away. The procedure worked well, despite occasions of bad visibility.

It was at Bainton, too, that I first heard of the combination of supervision of two stations under one Station Master, in this case Kipling Cotes and Enthorpe. Kipling Cotes was on the York-Hull line, while Enthorpe was on the Selby-Bridlington route. My recollection of this 'talked about' new-style economy was associated with the story that the Station Master concerned, who rather liked a 'jar', usually could not be found when telephoned. He was always 'on duty' cycling between stations where, en route, was his 'local'!

It was the practice for the District Managers to move staff around so that they gained experience, so in September 1923, eight months after arriving at Bainton, I was ordered to Foggathorpe on the Selby-Market Weighton line. My first consideration was, 'I'm not likely to find such an excellent lodging place as I had at Bainton'. And so it was. I was faced with having to stay at the local pub since there was no one else willing to accommodate a railway clerk. The prim and proper Station Master, the opposite of Mr Welburn, pointed the way, and that was that. Pubs were foreign to my upbringing, but I made the best of it, sleeping in a room immediately above the swinging sign which creaked away many a waking hour! I disliked the 'beery' atmosphere of the then rough village inn, and spent my 'off' evenings in the office studying railway accounts and block signalling. This earned the commendation of the Station Master and he even offered his help, which I appreciated. On returning to the pub, I would be in time to see a huge unshaven bulk of a man, formerly a textile millionaire, and now living on a large farm nearby, being shoe-horned into a buggy with the pony having its head set in the right direction and being verbally instructed to take its owner home! That happened every night of the week and evidently it worked, since he turned up each successive evening for more! The old boy did not sit in the bar but in the domestic 'snug' to drink, another reason why I could not spend my evenings there, as his company was to say the least unsavoury.

On Selby market day, the local farmers' wives and other women producers took their produce, poultry (live and dead), rabbits, vegetables, eggs, etc, on the train. Certain goods, and others over a specified weight, had to be charged what was known as 'excess'. This was a medley of traffic most difficult to assess, and what a variety of dodges there were to avoid payment! The Station Master, a wily man, taught me the ropes and I began to pit my wits against the offenders – and enjoyed the process. Another dodge was perpetrated by passengers wanting change, who offered a one pound note for a $3^1/2$d ticket. One evening, when the Station Master was at the ticket window, he was offered this, the passenger saying that he was sorry – and so was the SM. With a sly wink at me, he started to count out the change in coppers, clanging the coins on the desk top, a sound the passenger did not like. At 15 shillings the passenger said he would have another look in his pocket and with well-feigned surprise he 'struck oil' – or rather some coppers – and saved the day!

Against the same rail traffic on the wolds of grain, the predominant loading here was trussed hay and clover, the station being surrounded by fertile meadowland. This traffic, destined for less fertile areas for cattle and horse fodder, demanded the use of large-capacity vehicles such as double-bolster wagons, which were really built for the conveyance of steel, and it was most difficult to obtain them to meet farmers' requirements. This hay traffic had to be loaded carefully to keep it within gauge and required experienced men to obtain the maximum benefit.

These loads, when being removed by the 'pick-up', had to be passed under the 'loading gauge', which was a permanent structure at the exit to the yard. Such gauges were provided in most goods yards and were composed of a strip of steel curved into an arc and suspended over the track. If loads passed clear beneath the gauge, they would clear all tunnels and bridges en route.

It was not a very profitable traffic, but in line with the 'common carrier' practice at that time, a service had to be provided to meet the farmers' needs. If the loaded wagons were being sent to a station on a railway other than the North Eastern, usually referred to as a 'foreign' line, a debit was raised on the ropes securing the load, so that the receiving station had to return them in order to clear the debit – this is just one example of the intricacies involved.

Foggathorpe was on a double line, a change from my previous stations, and I therefore was able to learn more about signalling practices. Life could have its dramatic moments even here. A derailment of a double-bolster wagon at the yard entrance, blocking a down main line, gave me my first insight into single line working, and the interesting process of a steam crane re-railing the offending wagon. On a more human note, the central meeting point of locals on winter evenings was the blacksmith's shop – warm, no cost, free speech. It was this free speech which on one occasion proved too 'free' and tempers rose in argument. A bare knuckle fight developed between two huge farm-hands, which had to be stopped when one of them angrily picked up a horse-shoe and flung it at his opponent. This man ducked and fortunately it went wide, missed a spectator by a hair's breadth and went through the window. The blacksmith, 'a mighty man is he', soon swept them out of the arena.

In February 1924, the Brafferton Station Master, who had had some staff trouble, asked if I could be transferred back to him. Of course I was delighted, and back home I went. Now with a somewhat more mature approach, I found myself settling in to a routine, so I welcomed yet another change when I was requested to take up duty in the goods office at Boroughbridge, the next station towards Harrogate. It was a larger station, with certain shifts at the passenger office, but I was still able to live at home, though this meant cycling across fields on a bridle path, the site of the White Battle (1319). This route would sometimes flood, in which case I had to cycle 8 miles via Helperby, and for a 7 am start this meant an early rise.

The Station Master, Mr Cawood, lived in a superior detached house, built when the line between Boroughbridge and Pilmoor was opened in 1847. Mr Cawood had been in York headquarters in a senior position, but having suffered from poor health he was advised to take a country station, a job he welcomed and performed most conscientiously. Having a large coal sale he also came out satisfactorily financially in the transfer. He had a teenage family with whom I soon became acquainted, and I enjoyed working there.

The goods yard was a large area of sidings, loading docks, warehouses and the goods office, situated some five minutes' walk from the passenger station. There were three clerical staff in the goods office. The chief clerk, Grade 4, which I regarded as a very important post, was a Leeds man named Gregory, considerate and helpful with a strict sense of duty. Another clerk was called, strangely enough, Hicks (same as mine but with an 's') – gentlemanly and courteous in face of any provocation, a standard quite beyond me. The desks in the office were high and sloping and you either stood to work or sat on a high stool. There was a constant stream of people coming and going, while the cart-weighing, used for the coal trade and other checking purposes, and which had its reading mechanism in the office, needed frequent attention. The yard operations also called for some attention, and one of my regular jobs was to accompany the yard foreman into the large warehouses to check up on the goods on hand to compare with the office records – in other words, to make a meticulous inventory of what was on hand waiting for delivery or dispatch.

To describe fully the duties of the clerical staff at a station such as Boroughbridge would take too much space. Suffice to say that the laborious job of charging (based on the General Classification of Merchandise handbook) and invoicing outward traffic from completed consignment notes, and checking up with the outside staff that the goods were as described, occupied a lot of time. Advising consignees of the arrival of inward traffic by letter post was also time consuming, especially with full wagon loads when it had to be made clear that demurrage charges would be levied if the traffic was not removed by a given date. Collecting these demurrage charges was an even greater chore, as there was such resistance to these extra costs. Dealing with claims for damage and loss of goods, answering requests from the public re possible forwardings, cartage, payment of accounts, compiling monthly accounts, paybills for staff and so on, all provided work in the office in addition to items mentioned elsewhere. Anyone with a bicycle, like me, was used to collect outstanding accounts, those culprits most likely 'in the red' being located up difficult country lanes, or through muddy farmyards! And always a dog guarding the back door, a disgruntled pig mooching around, and the farmer's wife without any money!

The total staff of the station was Station Master (Class 3), two passenger clerks (Class 5), three goods clerks (one Class 4, two Class 5) one yard foreman, two porter signalmen, and two goods porters. The freight traffic was similar to Brafferton but on a much larger scale, and there were many more 'smalls' which were handled from the collection and delivery point of view by a hired carter who, with his horse and wagon, was under contract to work within a given radius of the station. Passenger and parcels business was of a wider variety than I had previously experienced so I had a lot to learn in those respects. But meeting the public here was of some special significance. The farmers were doing business on a large scale and demanded a lot; they could be most difficult when wagons were not available for them or goods were delayed. My village vernacular helped when I had learned to use it diplomatically, and my colleagues taught me a lot in this respect.

Every Monday there was a livestock market at Boroughbridge adjacent to the station, where cattle, sheep and pigs were exchanged either for slaughter or for further growth. It was one of the largest markets in the north of England and most of the animals went away by rail. It was a familiar sight to see the market conditions, for when I worked on a farm I used to drive all kinds of livestock 5 miles from my village to Boroughbridge market, see them sold and walk back in the evening. On the way out the animals were encouraged to drink as much as possible and so enhance their weight, the measure on which they were valued!

We would have one and sometimes two fully loaded trains with a total of 60 to 80 wagons of livestock for dispatch – high-revenue traffic. These trains went to Starbeck where the individual wagons were sorted and dispatched to wherever they were destined. Most went to the West Riding – Leeds, Bradford, Keighley, Halifax – while others went to York, Sheffield or the North. Inward livestock was spasmodic, being composed of cattle from Ireland or sheep from sales in Scotland.

Each consignment of animals had to be invoiced, with the correct number in each wagon. It was here that I first heard the old shepherd's quip that the railway checker always counted the number of legs going up the gantry and divided by four to get the true number! I was not allowed to forget the day I made a real faux pas. We used to send cattle to Bradford and also to Keighley – the trouble was that there was a customer named Keighley at Bradford. Inevitably, one day Mr Keighley's cattle were sent to Keighley and they missed this butcher's sales programme in Bradford! I had to meet him at the following market and apologise, and in true

Yorkshire style he presented me with a joint of best sirloin steak!

The farmers in the Boroughbridge area grew enormous acreage of potatoes, all of which produce was sent by rail. One farmer would order five 10-ton wagons for loading on a single day. His men would arrive at the station with their horses hauling double-shafted four-wheeled wagons full of 8-stone bags of potatoes; they picked them up and slung them into the wagons like toys, while our men counted them in (sometimes!). The yard was alive, the bantering loud, and the language basic! This went on from October to spring, when, in the reverse direction, many wagon-loads of seed potatoes imported from Scotland brought considerable revenue to our accounts, as the consignee was debited with carriage charges.

It was a common sight to see bolster-type rail wagons loaded with dressed trees (designated in the goods classification as 'round timber') *en route* to timber yards with rail connections. Boroughbridge had its share of loading this unruly commodity, when forest giants 35 to 40 feet in length were dealt with. Horse-drawn timber wagons brought in these large and heavy trimmed trees, oak, ash, beech and sycamore. Such movements had to be pre-planned; bolster wagons, the bigger the better, had to be ordered from Starbeck, and a gang of timber loaders, men trained in this work, booked through District Office to handle, load within gauge, secure and take responsibility for making them safe for transit. The loading had to be performed where the fixed station crane of 15 tons capacity could be used for the lifting process.

There was in Boroughbridge a maltings which operated under the name of Sadlers, with whom there was an exchange of traffic – raw barley coming in and barley offal, called 'sharps', going out, the latter being used for cattle feed. Also, a substantial brick and tile business emanated from a brickyard down the line in the Knaresborough direction owned by Greens, near the village of Roecliffe. It was a busy yard, their products being sent to a wide area, mostly to the West Riding, and practically all by rail. They were part of the Strensall Greens firm, so there was a certain amount of interplay and exchange between the two. But we had wagon supply problems with them at a time when wagon stocks were already in short supply. There were problems also with breakages of tiles, and it was difficult to assess and check the evaluations that the firm claimed from breakages. I had a number of visits to make to see the manager, a disabled man named Sutcliffe, who knew his job from A to Z in the settlement of disputes – you had to be well prepared to deal with him!

As a matter of interest, the railway owned the Boroughbridge to Ripon canal and maintenance of the lock gates had to be watched. Our informant was one of the station porters, George Johnson, who was the official lock-keeper and lived in the lock house. He was a man of many parts, a funny man and a 'skiver', but you couldn't help but like him!

Saturday was the cleaning-up day, when the goods yard closed at noon and the permanent way staff, the lengthmen, tidied up at both stations. They swept the platforms, cleaned up any nuisances, emptied the bucket-type toilets which were common at many stations, and maintained a high standard of cleanliness.

In the autumn of 1924, while at Boroughbridge, I met a Mr Howard Robinson, a friend of the Vicar of Myton, who was a founder member of the Merseyside Section of the Institute of Transport (having recently been formed, in 1919) and he suggested that I join the Institute, which was in London. I duly qualified as a Student and was admitted, very soon becoming a founder member of the Leeds and District Section which became the Yorkshire Section. Little did I think that I would become President of the Yorkshire section and a member of the council of the Institute for two years. Indeed, in 1991, now a Fellow of the Chartered Institute of Transport, I shall have been a member for 67 years.

Meanwhile I was continuing my studies of the subjects common to the general activities at a country station, in Goods Accounts, Passenger Accounts and Train Signalling and Rule Book procedures. I duly passed in all three, but it was the signalling and rule book subjects which proved the most complicated and difficult. However, I passed the written examination at a fortuitous time, just before the General Strike of 1926. I say at a fortuitous time because the strike brought out most railway staff, but I could not bring myself to join it. Still at Boroughbridge, an appeal was made, when signal boxes were left unmanned, for anyone who would undertake to work in one to volunteer, especially staff who had a knowledge of Rules and Regulations and train signalling. Here was my chance to put into practice something I had found difficult in theory, so I found myself allocated to work Knaresborough Goods Junction, the box controlling the junction with both the goods yard and the Pilmoor branch. The Station Master there spent some time with me showing the layout and lever movements.

The bell signals and indicators were easy as I had been used to those at stations where I had worked. I had as my assistant a bookmaker's clerk, more for company than for practical help. There were few trains, and those which ran were worked by crews composed of engineers, retired staff – anyone with some knowledge of the requirements. I found it exciting, especially the walk from Knaresborough station to the signal box to take up duty. I had to traverse the line in a cutting which was overlooked by many railway staff on strike, and they pelted me with anything they could lay their hands on, bottles, stones, anything, which caused me to take evasive action and run for it!

There were no goods trains and each passenger train possessed an atmosphere of gaiety with its passing, flags flying, waving of hands and cheering – not very professional, but it worked. I think I was sorry when it finished and I had to return to my normal duties. An entry appeared in my career history, 'Remained loyal and volunteered for other work', a step taken by management without precedent and never taken again after a union dispute. May I say that I was brought up in a 'blue' atmosphere in a 'blue' village, and did not agree with the strike. I was not a member of a trade union, and enjoyed dodging the brick-bats. Most of all I had an innate loyalty to my employer. I was thankful I had a job I liked, having been rescued from a drab life with no future.

It was at about this time that massive road works, remetalling the A1 in the Boroughbridge area and for many miles on each side, called for roadstone from

Wensleydale which was delivered through the station. It poured in, and redundant war transport vehicles were used to convey the traffic from station to road site, creating turmoil in our goods yard and elsewhere. As the road work progressed northwards, the flow of stone moved to other stations – that is how the A1 began to assume greater importance as a trunk road and how road improvements were assisted by rail in those days.

It was during this busy time that I had a contretemps with the Station Master, who could be very 'distant' if rattled. It was necessary for me to get in touch with the passenger clerk on duty, and there was a domestic telephone between my office and his. I kept ringing and ringing with no response until I pressed the sounding bell continuously. Eventually there was an answer and I rapped out, 'Are you damn well asleep?' Reply – 'How dare you speak to me like that?' – the gruff voice of the Boss. I had some difficulty in smoothing that one over!

So when, in the following week, the District Goods Manager at Leeds (in whose department I was) visited us on a periodic inspection, I anticipated a cold reception. Not so. He approached me and said, 'Do you want promotion Hick?' On answering in the affirmative, 'of course', he went on to ask, 'Would you like to go to York headquarters?' What more could I want? Evidently Mr Cawood had interpreted my earlier impatience to my advantage! Within two weeks I was in the headquarters offices at York.

The position was not so romantic or glittery as I imagined. Apparently headquarters were asking the district for suitable clerks to be taken into the rates office where there was to be a national revision of charges, especially the 'exceptional' rates, on all traffics between all relative points. The 'rates' office was the centralised point at which all these charges and the basic policies were decided for the North Eastern Division in conjunction with other centres throughout the country.

3.

JOINING THE BOWLER-HAT · BRIGADE

As may be imagined, the prospect of going from a somewhat lowly station job to a post in headquarters was fascinating. It conjured up some exaggerated thoughts, feasting the ego. There were congratulations from the Boroughbridge station staff and the Station Master's attractive daughter. At home, words of caution, advice on conduct, reference to swollen heads and size of hats! It meant leaving home at 7 am to cycle 5 miles morning and evening to and from Tollerton station to place me in York before the starting time of 9 am. Finishing time was 5 pm, working mornings only on Saturdays. Good holidays, extended bank holidays, improved working conditions – all part of the future picture. And the office. What an office! I had of course seen it before but now I was to work in it. It was in a spacious block, Georgian style, of a design and construction of outstanding merit, which had been completed less than 20 years earlier. A modern edifice, with beautiful woodwork and panelling, an impressive entrance and 'marble halls'. I just had to stop and marvel at it, and in so doing could not miss the coloured coat of arms engraved on the outside of the building, under the Chairman's room window on Station Road, which intrigued me. Representing the three constituent companies which formed the North Eastern Railway company in 1854, it included the coats of arms of the York & North Midland Railway, the Leeds Northern, and the York, Newcastle and Berwick.

On reporting, I was directed to an office holding about 30 staff, all employed on 'rates' work, and all installed at high sloping desks complete with stools. Working within the ambit of the General Railway Classification of goods rating, many of the men, who had a specialised field in which to work (eg steel, chemicals, agricultural products, livestock, etc) preferred to stand much of their day, since all telephoning had to be done from a centralised point. Receiving warmth in cold weather was achieved by a 'backside to fire' manoeuvre, so all in all there was much movement away from the desk seats! All the rooms in the building were heated by large coal fires with a modicum of central heating from radiators at strategic points.

My first impression was that I was being thrown into a maelstrom of technical 'buzz-buzz'. I was mystified, but new friends came along and soon I became part of

38

the establishment. One thing was certain, I had to dress differently now that I had joined the 'nobs' – dark suit and tie, black shoes and spats, black bowler-hat. Cycling along country lanes to and from the station in this outfit was no mean sight! Comic – or grotesque! My work consisted of copying exceptional (ie non-standard) rates per ton into certain documents as supplied to me by a rates clerk. No smoking was allowed in the office, but this clerk like many of his colleagues used to sniff 'snuff' at frequent intervals. I learned many facets of rate making including statutory charging and 'common carrier' obligations, and the basic thinking, the economics, behind this pattern of activity. Mileage, weight, operating cost elements and 'What the traffic will bear' (Ackworth) were all ingredients to be assessed and evaluated – overall it was a monumental job, especially when it is appreciated that practically all goods traffic for distances beyond horse-and-cart range went by rail. I learned of the deals and pressures at high level concerning major traffics such as steel, coal, bulk liquids, chemicals and cement, and of the railway officers who became negotiators in this field. Mineral traffic, eg coal, was dealt with by a separate charges section. I remember in particular Mr C.K. Bird leading the rates office as a young man – he later became General Manager of the Eastern Region. This was another angle to my transition in environment; I saw daily people in high places in the railway service and discovered that most of them were, after all, just ordinary human beings!

But to return to the 'Rates Revision', it had been called for by the Railways Act of 1921, described, as I well remember, as the most important Act relating to railways ever passed. I have heard that story a few times since then, but in truth this Act gave the Ministry of Transport – a new government department at the time – very wide powers over railway activities, and it was interesting to study its implications. Established by the Act, the Railways Rates Tribunal supervised and, one might say, controlled the level of charges for merchandise by rail which had to be worked out to a formula they laid down. The General Railway Classification of goods by merchandise trains, as it was known, the 'bible' I had worked on in its earlier simple form at country stations, was to be completely revised. It was hoped that this would reduce as far as possible the proliferation of 'exceptional rates', ie special quotations for specific traffics between two points. In fact, as it transpired this new structure failed in this respect.

The number of classes of merchandise listed in the GRC was increased from eight to 22, and this conversion had to be interpreted for every station where freight traffic was handled. Each station therefore had to keep for charging purposes, and public inspection if necessary, books showing the chargeable distance from the station giving the appropriate detail. Printed copies of the GRC and the schedule of standard charges in force had to be kept for sale by every railway company.

This, as will be appreciated, loaded a gargantuan task on to the Rates office at York. All stations concerned in the North Eastern Division of the LNER had to be provided by NE headquarters with an individual book applicable to that station. The mileages and other key information were provided by the main 'rates' office from existing records. So, the 30 clerks, including myself, were recruited from outstations, and located in a large shed in the 'Old Station' yard, and it was to this shed that I was directed to help with the work.

This shed was on the site of the present Hudson House, and our boss was a clerk of Class 4 status! A group of four clerks took a geographical area, entering up the books station by station as the details were fed to them from the rates office proper. I joined one of the groups and I am afraid that it was not the sort of work to generate enthusiasm. In fact, as nearly all the staff were young men, they tended to 'skive' at times, but for a period of about nine months they worked cheerfully, and a camaraderie emerged which lasted for many years. Anything to divert attention from the routine was seized upon, and there was a frequent procession of events centred on the city walls which were in full view of our hut (which we called our 'Tin Tabernacle'!). During the summer many young couples walked the city walls and, thinking they were out of sight, occupied an alcove. The activities in this alcove were far too distracting to miss, and the cry 'Alcove!' brought the office to a stand. All part of life's education.

When the 'appointed day' arrived, 1 January 1928, and the mission was completed, the staff were dispersed, many going back to country stations, but I was retained at headquarters and directed to the Traffic Statistics Office. In considering my position at this stage in the 'twenties, and surveying my career prospects, I felt I must try to stay in headquarters, which meant that I was to be parted from the commercial side of business. This I did not like, as I had become interested in the work and in the people. I felt as though I was surrendering something. I really had no concept of what 'traffic statistics' work involved, any more than I had of the wider railway world or of its industrial impact. That was to come later.

My scene was still the village scene and it was of great importance to me and, in my eyes, to the railway also. Hundreds of villages relied on their railway connection for transport and communication. Almost every station had a Station Master and supporting clerical staff, and every member of the staff at these country stations was concerned with dealing with people, with passengers and with their goods, charging for services rendered, looking after the 'shop', and handling the technical side of running the trains – a world apart. It was all part of the social structure and culture of the rural areas. The wrestling with the General Classification of merchandise, the click of the ticket-dating machine, the weighbridge demands, the clang of the bell signals in the signal box, the tick-tack of the single needle Morse telegraph instrument, the smell of the fish-boxes and the sniff of smoke from the 'tanky' hauling the local train – these were all part of the atmosphere which was still with me.

But round the corner there were changes pending. Post-war (1914-18) lorries were in evidence making short journeys with freight, farmers using them for conveying some of their farm produce, and buses infiltrating with their local passenger services and encouraging the 'locals' to cast their eyes towards the towns! This infiltration, denuding the local branch line trains of their traffic, started the rot. Daily we were being made aware that a new era was dawning in transport, and a new challenge to this monopoly for which I worked. I set off to a new job with some defiance, but with confidence!

The Traffic Statistics Office, or TSO as it was known, was the calculating centre for the traffic departments. Its machinery was elementary, so an army of staff was required to prepare the statistics then coming into prominence as a management tool. I went to the 'wagon-miles' section, composed mostly of girls working from freight guards' journals, producing the 'wagon-miles' figures which were coupled to other figures for the use of the operators. The mileage run by trains as recorded by each journal was calculated, written on each section of the journal, and for each stage of the train working the number of wagons between each mileage point was inserted. The number of wagons was then multiplied by the miles and a total of wagon-miles for each working, each day, was available – all calculated by simple mental arithmetic – and a key statistic was produced, followed by a marrying up with train engine hours to produce an important measure of working. Sadly, I found this work most depressing and after being discovered 'shinnanakin', I was put on the transfer list. However, I lived to appreciate more fully the figures which came from the TSO . . .

4.

THE 'SUPER'S' OFFICE

Where was I to go? I did not want to be ignominiously sent to a country station again, so I fished around for a possible job in the Operating department, already the place I was ambitious to reach. I heard that, as a result of staff economies, some girl typists attached to various sections of the office were being dispensed with and youths appointed in lieu. My typing, and much more my shorthand, was very questionable, but I took a chance and was appointed to the Programme department of the Superintendent's office. This department was where excursion and special passenger trains (including Royal Trains) were timed and included in the weekly working notice issued to all staff involved in carrying out the operational work. The geographical area covered at that time by this office was approximately from and including Tees-side in the north to Shaftholme Junction, almost as far south as Doncaster, and to the west within the compass of the former NER railway. Another Programme office based on Newcastle, but under the York headquarters' operating chiefs, covered the northern section up to Berwick. Later that office was transferred to York and the functions of the two activities combined.

I duly reported to the person in charge, one Hedley Sawyer (usually known as 'Uncle'), a forthright and very capable man who called a spade a spade. He was then a bachelor – grey moustache and smartly dressed in a grey suit, trilby hat, umbrella or walking stick – commuting by tram from and to Acomb. Originally from the wolds area of Yorkshire, he had retained much of the dialect, and many native figures of speech were trotted out in his daily commentary. What he interpreted as a weak theory or explanation would be described to him as 'a tale of a tub'; and someone being difficult over a proposition or project was 'the nigger in the woodpile'. Many synonyms, highly expressive, were quoted daily. At our first introduction he questioned me on my ability to write shorthand and to type – straight to the jugular, my weakest point – and when he realised the truth he rang the chief staff clerk saying that it was 'not on' sending him someone without proper qualifications! Apparently he was persuaded to give me a trial and, by pounding away on the typewriter every spare minute, and doing shorthand in my imagination on my bicycle or in church on a Sunday during the sermon, as well as on paper, I eventually satisfied him, though I had some apprehensive moments.

The day I arrived I was entertained by a typical interchange between the boss and one of his staff. Bill Hunter was raising his voice to someone on the wall telephone, and 'Uncle' shouted at him: 'Hunter – you know very well a soft answer turneth away wrath'. Hunter replied, 'Yes sir – I have just given him a really "soft" answer!'. Apart from the more senior men, the staff were all addressed by their surname.

In the 1920s the public timetable did not change a great deal. Regular trains were scheduled and the timetable compiled in the 'Timetable section', a joint affair between Operating and Commercial (Passenger Manager). The excursion and special trains, however, were dealt with in the Operating department, working on the one hand to the requirements of the Passenger Manager's excursion section under Ernest Whitfield, and on the other to the needs of the operators for reliefs, special movements (ie military moves), running of empty stock trains etc. Up to the start of the Second World War this traffic was most significant, proposals coming from the District Passenger Managers or initiated in Mr Whitfield's office, and designed to bring in good revenue. The projects might be for excursions to seaside resorts, day, half-day or evening trips to events of all descriptions (races, shows, football matches, lights), many of them at weekends, so in the summer and on Bank Holidays locomotives, coaching stock and line occupation were heavily committed.

Producing the weekly working notice (referred to as the 'programme'), printed at Ben Johnson & Co Ltd of Micklegate Works (now at Poppleton), was likened to meeting the constraints and time demands of a small edition of a Fleet Street newspaper. Time was of the essence. The outside staff must have the document in time for them to make their proper dispositions of staff and equipment, and despite the extra staff imported into the office in spring and summer, when holidays and better weather prompted a resurgence of activity, considerable overtime had to be worked to cope with requirement. Bank Holiday and other peak programmes could consist of over 200 pages.

A daily commitment was the issue to stations and others concerned of a special notice of trains and other movements not included in the weekly programme, by means of 'multiplex advices' – there could be 10 to 20 notifications per day, all being dispatched to stations and depots with a request to acknowledge receipt. The detailed timings, composition of trains and other instructions had to be set out in recognised form, typed on a wax sheet with a note of the number of pages required, then rolled off by the multiplex machine, worked, of course, by hand. The staff who had prepared a dispatch list then folded the advices, addressed them, and took them to the sorting office for forwarding by the domestic rail postal service. The workings so dealt with included short-notice requirements such as duplicate excursions needed as a result of heavy bookings on the parent train, reliefs for timetabled trains, officers' specials, fruit and other seasonal demands, emergency arrangements due to accident, engineering works, storm damage, etc.

Such trains were a large and important slice of railway working and revenue, involving the use of a great deal of equipment, often calling on the dregs of coaches and locomotives, yet they constituted to some extent the outward and visible signs of doing the utmost to increase income. Imagine, an evening excursion from York to Scarborough in midsummer for 1 shilling return – 40 miles there, 40 miles back. Popular while it lasted but weather and the passing of a phase resulted in a relatively short life.

The measure of success or otherwise was, I believe, simply an estimation of receipts taken from the number of passengers carried by each train. No real costings were then available – a full train was a good train. After each event an inquest was held by the responsible party, and an assessment made, the results from which determining whether to repeat the exercise, vary it, or reject any further trip. Often those inquests took place on a Monday morning in the form of discussions between 'Uncle' and Ernest, whose dedication to their cause had to be seen to be believed, and the programme staff were infected by their enthusiasm!

Many special trains for events throughout the region found support, quite apart from the regular excursion programme. Races in the North East attracted custom, and places such as Redcar and York, very popular meetings, had a programme to themselves. Trains with race enthusiasts for York were dealt with at a special platform near the racecourse (Knavesmire) at Holgate, and on such days crowds of people thronged the station proper as well. Similarly, Redcar had a special platform, and the resources on Tees-side were strained to the utmost. Excursions were also run to Hull for the fair, and Blackpool Illuminations drew enormous crowds by rail from the North East.

Specials were run to convey seasonal Scottish herring staff from Aberdeen to Scarborough and Hull, and further trains to Yarmouth and Lowestoft, following the herring shoals south, completed the sea harvest. Additional traffic came on to the railway after the fish was cleaned, through wagon loads being conveyed by passenger train to destinations all over the country.

Excursions to and from agricultural shows, such as the Royal Show and the Yorkshire Show, indeed almost any sizeable event, attracted excursion support as the railway often provided the only means by which most people could get a day out.

My duties included taking turns in the letter sorting and dispatch of all the sections in the Superintendent's head office which gave me a knowledge of how the functions were allocated and how the organisation worked. It also brought me into contact with colleagues from other than my own section. Being a junior meant being the lowest of the low, and one had to watch every point – a complaint was to be avoided at all cost. The most attractive room I found was the Central Control where an ingenious contrivance with five moving belts, driven by an electric clock mechanism at different speeds to represent train movements, portrayed the operating picture over the East Coast Main Line. This form of train control was a forerunner of the more sophisticated control systems which came along later. One could not experience anything more exciting than to watch the reports from signal boxes coming in to the controllers, delays being explained and recorded as they happened, and repercussions anticipated with appropriate instructions given to outside staff. A real exercise (to me at that stage) of 'playing at trains'!

I concentrated on my job, took examinations, and attended debating society meetings and other educational sessions. I attended Institute of Transport gatherings in Leeds and helped to form the Leeds and District Graduate and Student Society, soon to become its chairman. Then, after about six months in the section I welcomed 'Uncle's' decision to get a 'real' typist and place me on the desk where the manuscripts of the weekly working notices were prepared, and soon I was put in charge of this creative job.

The technique of setting out train and staff workings to the best advantage called for some imagination, and it was a most interesting occupation involving, amongst other things, close association with the printer and a knowledge of printers' methods. The handling of the information fed to me enabled me to accumulate a good knowledge of railway working practices throughout the system, including geographical constraints, staff dispositions and requirements, location, suitability and availability of locomotives and coaching stock, and the distribution problems associated therewith. Repercussions from wrong or inefficient scheduling or presentation were loud and clear from the man on the ground. It will be borne in mind that all branch lines and stations forming the old North Eastern were still in operation, with all their local services, heavy freight commitments, and the constraints of manually-worked points and semaphore signalling. Different forms of signalling (staff and ticket, tablet, etc), different train occupations of station platforms times of opening and closing, the physical layouts at each station – all these were items of importance on which my train working experience was being built. It would all be invaluable in the years ahead.

I reached the dizzy heights of temporary Class 4* when, in 1932, the northern office was brought from Newcastle and combined with the Programme office at York. In the ordinary course of events there was little promotion in the service and one applied for every Class 4 post as each vacancy list was issued, seniority in service counting for a lot. There arose a sense of desperation, and staff were leaving the service. It was, of course, a period of depression throughout the country and 'economy' was becoming a byword in the railway industry. Salaries and wages were constantly under revision and at one stage a reduction throughout the system was imposed, and accepted as a necessary move. At the same time, however, living costs were low, excursion fares low, and we were busy, but I felt I was getting bogged down as, try as I might, I failed to get a permanent promotion. I concluded that I had to do something different, so I wrote a paper on the work which took place in connection with excursion and special passenger train traffic, and its implications on railway business (the work, in fact, in which I was involved), and presented it to the Institute of Transport. Here is an extract from the Journal of the Institute, dated May 1930:

*The grading of clerical staff was: Junior (starting), Class 5 (on appointment), then Class 4, 3, 2, 1 and special.

LEEDS AND DISTRICT

Mr F.L. Hick (Student) speaking at a meeting of this society on March 21st last on the subject of 'Excursion and special passenger traffic', expressed the view that the cultivation of the travel habit had had the tendency to induce the public to regard a long distance as a detail. Race meetings, football matches, and similar attractions were, he said, attended by large crowds – which had to be conveyed to and from within a comparatively short space of time. This highly concentrated traffic was distinguishable from holiday traffic, inasmuch as the time of arrival at destination was not such an important factor, and might be spread over a longer period of time to suit operating requirements. There was other traffic which did not present serious difficulty in regard to density, and which might require a special train or, alternatively, could be accommodated by ordinary services.

The speaker discussed some of the difficulties encountered in arranging suitable running times for special trains; the subject of the 'working notice'; and the considerations involved in working highly concentrated traffic.

Other points touched upon included the provision of adequate indicators for the direction of passengers; the problem of ticket collection and the 'rationing' system adopted by the London Midland and Scottish Railway Company in connection with holiday traffic to and from Blackpool.

Finally, the speaker mentioned that the number of excursion passengers originating in the North Eastern Area of the London and North Eastern Railway and the receipts from such traffic for the year 1929 shewed an increase approximately of 20 per cent and 14 per cent respectively, over 1928. Such an increase, he contended, bore witness to the activity in the branch of railway working under discussion, and emphasised the growing importance of excursion and special traffic as a source of revenue to the railway companies.

I was awarded the 'Modern Transport Premium' prize for an original subject and it was quite exciting to be presented with a valuable set of books by Sir Josiah Stamp of LMS fame, then President of the Institute, in London.

I later prepared and read a paper to the Metropolitan Graduate and Student Society on 'The development of friendly relations between the public and the railways' as summarised in the following extract from the Institute's Journal dated January 1932. At about the same time I won a Railway Debating Society prize for a paper entitled 'The trend of modern signalling'.

METROPOLITAN

A meeting of the Society was held on December 1st, at which Mr F.L. Hick (Graduate) submitted a contribution on 'The development of friendly relations between the public and railways'.

At the outset the speaker contended that modern industrial conditions demand something more than the mere act of buying and selling. They demand a psychological influence which will dispel the usual rigid atmosphere of a hard and fast bargain and substitute a feeling of goodwill and satisfaction, as well as create in the parties concerned a mutual inclination to continue a cordial business relationship. The element of competition differentiates the conditions of the past from those of the present day and has revolutionised railway practice. It is this element which emphasises the truism that business can only be truly and permanently successful if its conduct is constantly and persistently directed to securing the satisfaction, goodwill and confidence of the customer.

It was the view of the speaker that the initiative for establishing satisfactory relations between the public and the railways must come from the railways, as the latter were in the position of producers requiring a market for their goods. The first essential to the development of a friendly relationship is efficient performance of contract. No amount of public relations work will influence traffic permanently to rail if the staff are indifferent to those who travel by train, and delays and breakages of a trader's goods are suffered in transit. Without good service, advertising and the offer of facilities are futile. A high standard of efficiency is necessary to gain prestige and beget confidence. A capable, courteous and helpful staff must be employed, and the most efficient methods of transportation utilised.

The following means whereby railways can keep in touch with the public were suggested: personal contact, press and publicity methods, discussion of common problems in committee, and personal contact was regarded as the most effective means of establishing satisfactory business relationships.

Committee representing single industries were indicated as an alternative to the local joint committees constituted under section 28 of the Railways Act, 1921. As an example of what could be achieved by contact through a committee references were made to the Shippers Advisory Boards Scheme in the United States of America and similar procedure in this country was advocated.

In 1933 I married someone special I had met in the Lake District (when she was 15 years of age and I 18), and we chose to live at New Earswick where I could use the train service to travel to and from York and even find it convenient to go home for lunch. (Hilda and I celebrated our Golden Wedding in 1983.) At 28 years of age my salary was £180 per annum, facing a maximum in the grade of £200 pa at 31 years of age! At this time it was conceded by many clerical staff that it was unlikely one would reach permanent Class 4 until after 30 years of age – in fact, a large proportion of men never left Class 5, and there could be over 100 applicants for each Class 4 vacancy. So I can truthfully say that my wife did not marry for either prospect or money!

I was keen on the Lecture and Debating Societies' work. Each main centre in the North Eastern had such a society, with membership composed of LNER staff, past and present, of all grades, the object being to discuss questions of general railway interest. Bringing the societies together with a body known as the 'Federation', which three times a year staged a major discussion chaired by a chief officer. It was at one of those meetings that I ventured into speaking, and afterwards Mr T. Bernard Hare, District Superintendent at Darlington and a recognised authority on railway operating matters, asked me to join him in a study group and submit a thesis on 'Line occupation'. I did this, and in 1936 he appointed me to his staff section at Darlington. I wanted a wide experience and, although I was to be appointed to a temporary Class 3 post in York, I decided to secure permanent status, even at a loss of income. I moved for an increase in salary of £10 per annum to my permanent figure, against a temporary loss of £20 pa. Big deal!

5.

OUT TO THE DISTRICTS – DARLINGTON AND YORK

My wife and I thus moved to Darlington, where our first son was born. After living in the pleasant garden village of New Earswick, where the environment was superb and where I had plenty of garden, enough to enable me to continue my beekeeping hobby which I had enjoyed from my early teens, my wife and I had doubts about finding a suitable alternative home in Darlington. Without really knowing, we had visions of being forced to accept industrial surroundings. Not so! We found a small property on the West side of the town above the banks of the river Tees, and came to love the area, with its proximity to Swaledale and Teesdale. However, we were in for a shock over the house.

We agreed with the owner to rent it, a normal practice at the time – mortgages were not easily available, especially to a penniless railway clerk! We had been established for about six weeks when, during breakfast, I observed two men taking down my garage (a wooden structure), and when I challenged them I was told it hadn't been paid for! I sent them packing, only to be told that my landlord was in financial trouble (and he a tax inspector) and either I had to purchase or get out. After my wife and I scraped out our pockets for the last few coins we could muster, we were able to find enough to buy, and this turned out very well in the end. But not before I received a bill for arrears in the tax on the property (a pre-war imposition), which I eventually overcame by sending the documents to the solicitor who had acted for me in the conveyance, and who should have seen to this before conclusion of purchase. He did not even acknowledge receipt, but there was no further demand. A good start!

I worked on various matters under the District staff clerk and sought as broad an experience as I could, dealing with workmen's compensation claims, personal accidents, and assisting with the desk-work on wages grade vacancies. I felt nearer the ground in a District Office and immediately wanted to be active in the train working, passenger and freight, and the signalling and safety sections of the office. The District Control was like a magnet to me, and out of office hours I studied the graphing systems of control, a scheme which Mr Hare had promoted in the North East. The Tees-side area was the largest steel-producing district of all railway originating centres in the country, with ICI at Billingham putting considerable traffic to rail. It was a demanding and busy freight district calling for first-class performance, and Bernard Hare, not everybody's favourite, met the challenge. I was pleased to be involved.

There was a very understanding and knowledgeable Chief District Inspector, George Henderson, who volunteered to prepare me for an oral examination in Train Signalling and Rule Book Regulations conducted by the Headquarters Chief Inspector. To secure an Inspector's job this was a necessary preliminary, and in due course I qualified. Not only that, but he allowed me to accompany him outside office hours to accidents and derailments where I became aware of the safety and other requirements necessary in these circumstances. I also saw the crane operations and what was involved under differing circumstances in the re-railing of a wagon, a coach or a locomotive, and rubbed shoulders with ground staff including locomotive people working on the job. It was all valuable experience which no doubt led Bernard Hare to ask me to take over temporarily the post of District Coaching Stock Inspector.

This involved getting out of the office and travelling to coaching stock depots in the District, and to stations where work such as carriage cleaning and inspection was being carried out. Coaching stock for main line and local train services had to be inspected frequently by an Inspector from District Office in addition to the Station Master concerned, and plans for a huge programme of excursion and special trains at weekends had to be checked. The allocation of vehicles to meet all originating requirements had to be carefully vetted and any movements of stock organised, making sure as far as possible that the Carriage and Wagon Engineer's staff had checked for technical fitness.

Cleaning was a vexed question, with complaints coming in continuously, while there were many difficulties with cleaning staff, some being inadequate in themselves or due to lack of proper facilities. It must be borne in mind that there were no mechanical appliances to assist them. The outside work was performed from ground level with long-handled brushes, while hand-brushes and elbow grease were employed inside. It was the Cinderella of the organisation, but it nevertheless had to be attended to as efficiently as possible, and pressure was exerted on the local supervisors to get the best results possible.

My job was to contend with the practical aspects of stock availability and control, geography, the date and time factors, layout and capacity of storage points, the composition of trains and technical constraints, through the time-honoured, sleight-of-hand, do-it-yourself method. And, of course, there was continuous liaison with headquarters coaching stock control, the over-ruling body which required co-operation and firm compliance with its instructions.

It was at about this time that the LNER was determined to improve in a spectacular way the image of the East Coast route to the North East and Scotland in the matter of speed and service. Trials had proved the capability of locomotive to achieve higher speeds. *Mallard* was creating records and the introduction of the 'streamliners' excited public interest and zipped up the morale of the staff. Darlington was on the direct route and Tees-side and Tyneside people were delighted with the innovation.

The 'Silver Jubilee' express was introduced in 1935 and it was with great pride that we railway staff pointed to this achievement. Its timing and outstanding design were to us a prediction of things to come. We never tired of referring to it in conversation and it was a favourite pastime to take our friends and acquaintances, especially, children, to see the train speed under one of the bridges south of Darlington. Its coaches and streamlined engine, of an overall silver colour, thrilled us. We would stand high on the bridge and see the 'up' silver streak approaching along the line, steam issuing from its chimney, panting and snorting under our very feet, and dashing forward as if eagerly anticipating the long straight stretch of high-speed line towards Northallerton and the south. It really was before its time – but the looming war was to kill it.

By the middle of 1938 I was getting restless. I had discovered that, when out on the line, I was concerned with 'real' railway work, and I wanted to be in that world. Eagerly I applied for a District Traffic Inspector's post at York, permanent Class 3, under my old boss's boss when I was at HQ, Lowingham Sproat. He was now District Operating Superintendent at York, and he wanted to see me. A tall man, meticulous, solid, with a deep sonorous voice, he put me through the mill. I was appointed, and I regard this move as the turning point in my career.

I immediately became involved first hand in the working of both passenger and freight trains, in the stations and in the marshalling yards. I was set a hard programme, my duties spilling across many activities over and above the level of the post, as by early 1939 traffic on the railways was beginning to build up on the rumours of war. I enjoyed every minute, even working weekends, particularly on the supervision of train working during engineering work. In supervising these operations (eg bridge repairs and renewals, permanent way renewals, relaying crossings, signalling renewals or repairs, etc) I had to ensure that all proper safety precautions had been planned and implemented. It was drilled into me from the start that it was during out of routine work of this kind that danger of accident was always present as a result of one of the many people involved making a mistake or omitting to observe the formula. Continuous vigilance was therefore necessary, and this checking-up process, in close collaboration with my colleagues in charge of the workmen, together with the key signalling staff, was my prime duty on these occasions. I was in charge, and safety on the line on the ground was my responsibility.

Every Saturday and Sunday in summer, when not employed on engineering work, I had the job of supervising and controlling the exceptional and extensive movement of excursion and special trains together with the ordinary service within the Scarborough area. I was stationed in Falsgrave signal box and directed priority of movement in conjunction with the signalman concerned. This included the transfer of coaching stock to and from day storage sidings at Gallows Close or further afield (eg Seamer), locomotives to and from the local motive power depot, sequence of train departures from the platforms, strengthening of trains, replacement of failed engines or failure of staff to appear. All this was quite beyond the Station Master's capacity, when taken with all his other commitments at the station on a busy pre-war weekend. Occasionally Mr Sproat would come to Falsgrave and 'listen in', giving support to our activities. And I, along with other staff, would return to York by the last train, weary but usually feeling that a good day's work had been done!

One particular incident comes to mind during the early days after my return to York. I was asked to take a gang of men (normally employed on loading timber) to a colliery in South Yorkshire where I was to off-load a heavy electric transformer (weighing some 3 to 4 tons) on to the colliery site adjacent to the sidings line. It was an extremely valuable and sensitive piece of equipment accepted by the sending station as 'delivered'; therefore it was the railway's responsibility to perform the delivery operation! When I saw what was involved, I realised that I had no suitable equipment, let alone 'know-how'. So I sought out the colliery foreman, one of those extraordinary practical men who literally run a works, and he came to my rescue. He could use my men of course, and with block and tackle, strong greased steel sheets and a strong arm, the transformer was skidded sideways inch by inch off the wagon to its site. Why should I remember this incident so vividly from amongst literally scores of predicaments a railway Inspector had to contend with? I think without a doubt that it was meeting, out of the blue and at the right moment, a man so capable in a practical sense, so willing to help, so ingenious, so rough with his orders to men working to his instructions, improvising and getting the job done. Really 'the salt of the earth'!

Anyone in the District Office who had a 'hot potato' on his desk was pleased to grab a District Inspector to help. One such case was the annual winter problem at the sugar beet factory at Poppleton near York, and at Selby where, during the peak intake (October to January), wagons of loaded sugar beet pile up in the sidings despite the loading permit scheme in operation designed to overcome this. Every year there occurred days of serious congestion on the one hand, or demands from the factory for wagons which were delayed somewhere en route. Occasionally full train loads of surplus beet had to be sent off to factories elsewhere to ease the position, and it was a harrowing job for the Inspector on site to meet urgent demands from all sides. The sugar corporation, quite naturally, had to keep on top of the work, running the factory continuously to achieve maximum production, and any faltering on the part of rail transport brought forth the 'big guns', when our commercial people had to use all their influence with the movement people to rectify the situation. On the railway side, wagons were at a premium and various devices were resorted to, out at the country stations, to satisfy their customers – the farmers – such as using coal wagons (also in short supply but accepted in some areas) instead of 'highs', or loading contrary to permit. Most of the sugar beet factories were on the eastern side of the country and, overall, beet was then a substantial traffic.

As 1939 progressed it was a time of premonition and fear. All realised that war was coming. It was also a period of increased industrial activity, the heavy trades demanding a considerably increased service from the railways. Steel-carrying wagons were at a premium, despite the increased stock, freight yards and the main lines were hyperactive, and steam locomotives were given impossible tasks to keep pace with operating requirements. A traffic Inspector, as an extension to the Operating offices, was always in demand and was expected to make recommendations to solve every problem! In addition, military requirements were taking precedence, and potential army needs meant close liaison with Northern Command which then had its headquarters in York. Troop movements were planned (under 'secret' headings) and one job I was asked to do was to visit every country station serving the North York Moors and detail on paper the facilities at each place for potential off-loading or loading of track and motorised vehicles by rail.

In addition, more traffic was passing which was out of gauge. Checking of loads was a frequent duty, as many inexperienced military and industrial staff were loading over-wide equipment on to rail wagons. Many weekends were taken up travelling with those difficult consignments to ensure correct working, checking that the load conformed to stated measurements, and ensuring, when it was *en route*, that Control, signalmen and trainmen were taking account of the restrictions involved. Some loads necessitated single line working or removal of ground ('dolly') signals, while others merely blocked the opposite line; but such a facility could not be made available except on Sundays, and some loads had to be staged week by week at progressive points. Such was the case with the huge out-of-gauge transformers from Parsons on Tyneside moving at frequent intervals to the south of England, all connected with the war effort and therefore of great importance.

The declaration of war obviously changed the whole outlook and emphasis of life, although railway-wise I have to say that the transfer of control to the Ministry of Transport was hardly noticed by me. Our second son was expected. Bombing raids were expected. I had to register for active service. I was told, however, that I was in a 'reserved occupation', and at the age of 34 was 'an old man', so that was that. But I did increase my 'off-duty' interests by more attention to the St John Ambulance Brigade, and I joined the Royal Observer Corps. I also did firewatching duty during air raid warnings when not with the ROC.

The effect of the war on the railways was nonetheless dramatic. From a warming-up process in 1938-39, traffic became an avalanche, the blackout, staff losses to the forces, shortage of wagons and the massive drain on other equipment adding to the pressures which put a strain on everyone. Also with this momentous swing of emphasis towards the railways, the provision of extra running facilities, marshalling yards and storage sidings became a major issue in which I became involved. Train and traffic controls had to be strengthened, while freight train offices needed to be fed continuously with information on what was happening outside, and given help.

I call to mind a particular freight panic caused by the petrol restrictions. All three breweries at Tadcaster feared that their distribution transport by road would be 'grounded', and asked for someone to see them with a view to all their production being transferred to rail at Tadcaster station. I had the job of seeing the top people, gathering the details of what they would like, and formulating a plan. A special train was organised for each evening to York marshalling yard where the beer wagons were transferred to trunk services to many parts of the country. However, air raids, blackout difficulties in the shunting yards and priorities in other directions caused many 'hiccups', and we were in difficulty. That beer caused more trouble than the whole military command. The brewers in any case expected more than we could physically give, but we had to show willing. Eventually they obtained some petrol, left us with the movements we could manage, and put the rest back on the road.

Immediately following Dunkirk I accompanied an ambulance train conveying men who had suffered in the evacuation. It was full of stretcher cases with accompanying medical and nursing staff, all bound for Scotton Hospital, Knaresborough. On arrival at Knaresborough it was dark, and there was a tunnel at the end of the platform into which the train had to project in order to place the ambulance vehicles in the right position. This represented a difficult manoeuvre, making sure that the train moved smoothly and strictly to order. Some of the casualties were serious and it was heart-rending to see the distress of some of the boys who had suffered at Dunkirk, who were in defeat and had experienced a long journey, first by rescue boat then nearly 300 miles be train. It was for me a first-hand introduction to the tragedy of war, in an emotional setting.

The immediate sequel was that I was taken home to York by car, driven by a titled lady (a recruited emergency driver), who had in the stress taken too much to drink. We were up the roadside bank a few times and scraped around corners on two wheels, and I was quite relieved to arrive home safe and sound. (I could not take over the car as I did not then drive!) The lady drivers of office cars came from all walks of life and they were really quite splendid. They worked shifts and had to turn out whatever the weather. But they had their moments – they easily disagreed amongst themselves and literally on occasion tore each other's hair, and they became the darlings (or the bane) of the lives of 'on call' Inspectors. They were not popular though, when, as was often the case, they had to rouse you during the night to attend an emergency, and in so doing woke the baby!

With the introduction of blackout conditions, the Inspector's lot was fraught with risks from stumping around in strange surroundings during darkness. On the running lines, in marshalling yards and at passenger stations where there was very dim lighting, avoiding pitfalls concentrated one's mind. I was provided with a handlamp (rape oil fed), but even so the railway environment always holds the unexpected for the unwary. On walking along the track I kept clear of running lines as far as possible, but when 'needs must' I chose the outside edges of the sleepers (not the middle of the track), which was not an easy manoeuvre at any time. I tramped many miles on sleeper ends visiting remote level crossings to check on safety factors.

Marshalling yards, where shunting was continuously in progress, called for great caution. Shunted wagons sometimes had a habit of running silently along the sidings and striking the unwary, so a knowledge of the movements in all parts was essential. During the hours of darkness, when some of the most intensive shunting took place, seeking information in detail could be a nightmare, especially if blackout conditions were coupled with frost, fog or snow and/or rain. Most hostile to the stranger.

Travelling on locomotives, as was sometimes necessary, with the cab hooded to conceal fire glare, was, especially when air raids were going on, an experience in itself, while accompanying the guard in his van on other occasions all added to wartime memories. I relied a lot on the advice and information given by an experienced guard – the drivers of our railway trains have appealed to the romantic and the enthusiast, but we should never forget the guard! I can only say again and again what valiant chaps those trainmen were, as indeed were all railwaymen working at ground level during those hazardous and uncomfortable days.

My memory also goes back to the dimly-lit passenger stations where, however one tried to warn them, travellers would inevitably be involved in an accident. White lines were painted along the edge of platforms to assist in identifying where the danger lay. Obstructions were marked, and steps had secluded lights focused on them. Platform and concourse lamps were hooded, giving a mysterious and sometimes sinister atmosphere, with shadowy figures flitting around doing what was in fact a simple routine job! Complaints still arrived in the office about delays or non-arrival of mail or of important parcels, and even small livestock, so I spent many all-night sessions at transfer points seeking the cause and the solution.

There was something about a winter's night on duty investigating a traffic problem at a large open station such as York or Leeds which left a chilling sensation, difficult to shake off. It was a cold job, and tiring. The long heavily loaded trains of 12, 16 or 18 coaches seemed to snake into the platform lines, coasting in on their 'stocking feet', silently, stealthily, as if hiding their purpose, full of reclining passengers, the majority of whom were service people. As much as one tried to keep in touch with train arrivals, and at the same time check on movements elsewhere, the silence and limited information would beat you. There was so much mail and parcels traffic to handle, much of it for transfer to other trains or to stand waiting departure time on other platforms, that porterage staff were kept fully occupied, and you were alone. Too much enquiry and there would be staff suspicion as to what was afoot. It was important therefore, as in any similar exercise, to seek their support at the outset.

But this experience with all its implications, when the aftermath of Dunkirk was also presenting a real possibility of invasion and was uppermost in people's minds, coloured my thinking, and left an indelible mark on my memory.

In January 1940 I was appointed to the post of Class 2 Signalmen's Inspector for the York area, the busiest in the District. This involved more attention to technical signalling and signalmen's duties. More than ever I had to attend accidents as quickly as possible after their occurrence, supervise the working, and report on cause and effect to the District Superintendent.

I had to be satisfied that at each signal box in my area the men were competent and were performing their duties in accordance with the regulations applicable at that box, and also that level crossing keepers, of which at that time there were very many, some of whom were women, understood what was required of them. I was required to visit every signal box and level crossing once a month and sign the train register book and 'occurrence book' to certify all was in order. My area included York station and yard, the main line north to Otterington (in which section Thirsk box was situated, the first British installation, opened in 1933, to include route setting by panel operation and relay interlocking by electric circuits), and the branch lines from Pilmoor to Malton and York to Market Weighton. All of this involved walking considerable distances where the train service was inadequate.

Every new signalman in my area had to be 'passed' by me as capable of working the box properly, and when it came to testing a man for one of the large boxes it faced me with a problem. For example, York Locomotive box, the largest manual signal box in Great Britain, had 295 levers and controlled the southern end of York station and the entrance and exit to the York marshalling yard. A new man had to be tested as to his knowledge of the traffic involved and his ability to interpret movements correctly and set the road accordingly. He had to work in conjunction with the senior signalman in the box who was known as the 'regulator'. I surmounted this difficulty by requesting my senior relief signalman, who himself could work the box, to put the new man through his paces and check his performance, working to my 'movement' requests, the 'regulator' also keeping an eye on the proceedings. It had to be borne in mind that usually men applying for these posts had already had a wide experience in other York boxes, before spending some considerable time 'learning', and jobs of a higher denomination were allocated on seniority and service. To sum up, a new signalman in any box had to prove that he was conversant with the interlocking of points and signals, track circuit limitations and the requirements for train working movements; the most stringent tests were made to ensure that he was proficient in all respects.

To this day I think of the 'regulator' at York Locomotive signal box standing for almost the whole of his shift, on the balcony protruding from the box over the track, issuing directions to the various signalmen whose duties were allocated to sections of the line. I have been there on icy cold, foggy nights when visibility was only a few yards, when he had to rely mainly on verbal reporting from the ground by guards, shunters, drivers or station staff, with no all-line track circuit diagrams in the box to guide him. Semaphore and 'dolly' signals with poor colour penetration during fog or darkness were the guide to drivers, guards and shunters, and clearance of points by trains or other movements had to be verbally reported if there was no visible tail lamp passing the box. Railway operating in the raw!

The work of signalmen in the important manually-operated boxes required a good physique to work the heavy levers which they had to handle, as well as a capacity to think clearly, and to interpret properly what was going on traffic-wise and what was required of them, perhaps in terms of dealing with an emergency, or solving a train working problem. Their knowledge of the signalling and safety regulations, at that time in many different boxes, and their ability to work the Morse single needle telegraph instrument were fundamental to the job, and I constantly marvelled at their contribution to the running of the railway. In the large boxes, boys were employed to record bell signals in the train register book, and it was a detailed task to interpret at a later date what had happened in sequence when a delay or accident had to be investigated. Those lads often later continued in the signalling grades, having learned much of the work as they went along; this provided a useful recruiting field. Occasionally a signalman would wish to enter the clerical control grade and, where appropriate, this was arranged.

As in many other aspects of the railways following the Second World War, the development of train signalling and related techniques was simply astonishing. Here, however, I have simply referred to some of my impressions as I experienced them in 1940 and with which I was so closely associated.

Marshalling yards and reception sidings were quite incapable of accommodating the trains presenting themselves at that time for sorting or forward working. The heavy flow of industrial products and the balancing flow of empty wagons to originating areas such as Tees-side, meant severe delays and long hours to trainmen. Those who had to read the Control graphs saw day after day long red lines denoting trains standing on running lines. Decisions had to be taken by the Controls (approved by senior officers) to block certain lines with loaded and empty wagon trains during the week as a backlog built up, being left for clearance at weekends when originating traffic subsided. As congestion threatened (or sometimes too late, as it occurred), embargoes were placed on traffic passing via certain routes and the code word 'Gosling' was a dreaded restriction indicating that no wagons should be loaded or forwarded to marshalling yards making up trains for the route concerned. Many storage points were used in and around the York area, notably the Picton-Battersby line and the Tadcaster–Wetherby line, which week after week were filled during peak periods and cleared on Sundays. To store this traffic, single line working over the branch lines had to be implemented, in order to keep the local passenger service running. A preponderance of goods concerned was steel traffic from West Hartlepool, Consett, Darlington and Tees-side flowing to the south and west. All Inspectors therefore at some stage or other were involved in this exceptional working. Two urgent 'new works' requirements were new reception and departure sidings at Skelton (York yard) and a new slow line over the river Ouse on the down side, works which were undertaken as priorities.

Meanwhile, isolated bombings by enemy aircraft caused upsets on various railway routes. During my period as Inspector for the main line north of York, I was called out to a bombed freight train between Raskelf and Pilmoor, about 18 miles north of York. It was a train-load of confectionery from Rowntrees chocolate factory to Faslane on the West coast of Scotland where there was a naval base – goodies for the Navy! The down fast and slow lines were blocked by derailed and damaged wagons, a low flying enemy plane having made a direct hit. Single line working was introduced over the up line (there was no up slow) to filter a few trains through on the main line. Diversion of most of the traffic was via Starbeck, Ripon and Northallerton (the Leeds Northern line).

The breakdown crane was brought to the scene and, working from the down main line, moved the damaged wagons on to the side of the line so that they were out of the way pending a more propitious time for final removal. At each move of the swinging crane, its jib fouled the up line, so the site had to be protected by a hand-signalman with detonators, each train approaching being warned at the signal box controlling the section to proceed with caution and be prepared to stop at the hand-signalman. It was dark and sleeting, the weather was utterly hostile and I and the staff working on the ground were up to our knees in chocolate and slush.

On arrival at the site I had satisfied myself that the hand-signalman was in position and understood that when the jib was swung it blocked the single line, and this would be indicated by a red light. The work was proceeding well when, to my horror, I saw a huge sizzling locomotive hauling a freight approaching through the blizzard, when the jib was fouling! It was coming slowly, but it was going to collide with the crane. I shouted and ran towards the oncoming train exhibiting a red hand-signal. The driver stopped 10 yards short of the obstruction, and when I climbed on to the engine I was told that the pilotman's warning has been given but there had been no hand-signalman and no detonators. It transpired that the hand-signalman had left his post to answer the call of nature and the detonator had failed to explode fully. The resultant domestic enquiry was interesting.

So often at this time I was in charge of an emergency when action had immediately to follow a verbal order. It was necessary to think quickly and clearly in advance of giving such an order which could set the staff on a sequence of events when time was of the essence. This experience also brought home to me the practical issues which had to be considered, such as the tendency of many staff to give far too optimistic forecasts of resumption of normal working, and the taking into account of the consequential effects of many seemingly unconnected directions. Each step therefore had to be carefully thought through; safety was the paramount concern, even though it very often proved a highly delaying ingredient. It taught me that skills in operating know-how could not be measured by mathematical process as though it was a true science. You had to relate to many experiences and many human traits which inevitably influenced what went on in each and every incident.

The movement of royalty and VIPs always required the presence of Inspectors at strategic points during wartime, and more will be told in this connection later. I was particularly involved when the King and Queen or other senior members of royalty were to be accommodated in the Royal Train overnight in the York District. The place selected for this was in a cutting to the south of Crimple Tunnel between Wetherby and Harrogate. It was chosen because it was away from possible bombing targets, it was in a cutting below surrounding land level, and if conditions required such, the train could be drawn into the tunnel for security. Also, there was no night service on the branch. The Royal Train was protected by the Army from intrusion, and an all-night watch was posted around the area. On a number of occasions I was the railway representative through whom all information had to be passed to the senior operating officer in the adjacent signal box. I was required to keep in close touch with the army officer in charge, who was in turn in telephonic communication with the air raid warning and other emergency services. All concerned with security were provided with a password which had to be offered if challenged. Only once did we have to consider drawing the train into the tunnel, and that was when there was a serious air raid on Hull and some stray bombs came in our direction. In the event we remained in position. This site was also used for Winston Churchill, and General Eisenhower. Winston's code was so apt – 'Rapier'.

A check on all the arrangements was necessary before the train arrived to ensure that the signalmen and other staff knew exactly what was required. The semaphore signals had to be in the correct position, the points likewise, the exact location of the 'stop' identified and men in position with detonators to protect the train after it came to a stand. The sanitary pans for placing under the train toilets, always a bone of contention by the staff who had to handle them, had to be checked when in position and confirmation given that the right number were available. Locomotive men were required to keep the engine in steam to heat the train when necessary, and all staff were on alert to permit movement should that be necessary.

My particular job as York Area District Inspector also carried with it the control of all relief signalmen in the District. A clerk did the programming of the duties, and subject to consultation with me, allocated the men to the jobs, weekly and on a seniority basis. Holidays, sickness, vacancies, special duties, all had to be catered for. A highly intelligent set of men, they needed careful handling, but once you got their confidence they proved to be the most loyal and supportive bunch of fellows one could ever wish to meet.

6.

WARTIME CONTROL

Towards the end of 1941 I was appointed Deputy Chief Controller in York District Train and Traffic Control. This meant working shifts and one weekend in three, indoors, and under pressure, but again right in the 'action' – running the railway! The geography and layout of running lines and marshalling yards and sidings were factors well-known to me, but more difficult to assimilate was the freight train pattern and the locomotive men and engine diagrams. There was also a flow of traffic figures to supply to Central Control and District Office, the compilation of which took into account the wider implications of the traffic situation of the North Eastern as a whole (in which the York District was a key area), and the national situation. What was happening at the Banbury exchange influenced the traffic flow back to Tees-side, with the York District playing a major part in decision making. Place names such as Banbury and Annesley became bywords in our vocabulary – we had never heard of them pre-war! – as did many other railway centres never built for the weight of traffic now thrown at them.

At York, the District and Central Control offices were located deep under the city walls opposite York station, placed underground for security reasons. Thus protected from blast, a direct hit by an explosive was the only risk of damage to these important communication centres. Train and traffic control had been greatly extended before the war and additional people brought into these offices. The main line Control had changed its name and function – it was now known as Central Control – and no longer had any direct control over train running, which had been taken over by the Districts. It was the centre point for inter-regional consultation and for co-ordinating the North Eastern as a whole on train and traffic matters, including exceptional wagon movements, embargoes on transits and keeping Operating chiefs fully informed on the current position. The District Controls had therefore assumed responsibility for the activities within their own area.

With the expansion of movements, the system of control had progressed from what might be termed an 'aide-mémoire' function to an effective authority, supported by an adequate telephone and reporting process between signalmen, yard and station staff, and the controller. Nevertheless, the recording of actual working was important, both to the controller and to the analyst who had to seek ways and means of improving results. The North Eastern, largely through the efforts of Bernard Hare, had adopted the 'graph' system. This called for the compilation, as the day proceeded and for each section of line for which a controller was responsible, of a record of the running of every train – black for movement, red for delay. The graph blanks were printed with the regular passenger train movements, using one document for each 24 hours, thus revealing at a glance, and at any time of the day, where the delayed occurred and the reason for it.

As Deputy Chief Controller (incidentally the Chief Controller was the Chief Trains Clerk in the District Superintendent's office) I had to supervise the whole operation, deal with problems associated with delays, derailments, major accidents and traffic congestion (the main ongoing problem), inter-district and bordering inter-regional contact, and keeping my seniors fully informed. It was important to ensure as far as possible that collieries were supplied with empty wagons and loaded ones cleared, steel-carrying wagons had to be chased 'up hill and down dale', freight guards' vans (of which there was an acute shortage at times and trains were therefore unable to move!) had to be searched for, and at times yardmasters or Station Masters had to be pressed to achieve the unachieveable. At the end of the shift there was the compiling of the 'log' for the boss, which called for all the literary and dramatic talent at one's disposal to give full vent to the real happenings of 8 hours in a wartime Control Office.

Air raid warnings were commonplace and Control relayed them to outlying areas. Reports of bombs having been dropped had to receive attention according to a laid-down formula, and similar treatment had to be applied to suspicion of unexploded bombs. On the night of 29 April 1942 I was on night duty when we received an alert, and from a good deal of publicity and foreboding in the newspapers about the Badaeker raids, we expected York to be the target. And so it transpired. We soon knew that the enemy had pinpointed the railway. The motive power depot was hit, a passenger train standing in the station was hit and set on fire, the telegraph and booking offices were wrecked and many bombs caused considerable damage in the city. I was thrown off my feet when the station was hit, thankful that we were several feet underground.

Soon we had to help the staff from the station who knew of our hide-out and who were in various stages of injury and shock. My friend John Grant appeared, dishevelled, battered and bruised, black, grim, unable to understand how he had escaped from a totally collapsed building. Many other less fortunate people were taken to hospital. Apart from personal repercussions, there followed the major work problem of re-routing trains to avoid York station, and other emergency arrangements to attend to which obviously fully occupied the Control staff. Senior people came in as soon as they could make their way through the bombed streets to assist while, outside, breakdown crane staff, signalling engineers and others concerned concentrated on restoring facilities. Everyone who could help rallied round, and outside Inspectors acted as additional support in whatever direction they were needed.

Instead of arriving home for breakfast at 7 am, I got in at 11 am, weary to say the least, having meanwhile called at the station and motive power depot to see the damage. And there the giant Gresley 'Pacific' locomotive *Sir Ralph Wedgwood* was lying, mutilated, destroyed, in a heap of ruin. A night to remember!

Such incidents were, of course, taking place all the time throughout the country, and unless one was personally hurt, a philosophical mentality developed, and people just 'had to get on with it'.

7.

FREIGHT INDIGESTION

After about a year as Deputy Chief Controller, during which I had made a number of recommendations with regard to freight train operation, I was asked to take a lateral move into the planning side of the District Office trains section. Delays were phenomenal, the long red lines on the control graphs being a daily reminder of the seriousness of the position. Trainmen incurred extremely long hours sitting on their trains in sidings, while slow running lines (or even main lines) and every 'bolt hole' were filled. So I was asked to assist in promoting a more efficient plan.

Fred Margetts was head of freight trains in headquarters and he directed the 'drive'. 'Drive' was the operative word, as anyone who new Fred was aware – few evenings free, no weekends free. My wife thought I had left home, since even many of my nights were also occupied with duty at the Observer Corps centre. Here I was on the top bench of operators, plotting our own and enemy planes in response to outside spotters and radar reports from the German coast, across the North sea, and into home territory. We could be excused for praying for a foggy night which grounded all planes!

It was satisfying to see improved results on the line by better planning both through timetable and marshalling yard reorganisation, together with better regulation discipline at the first sign of congestion. The co-operation of other Districts and Regions was essential, and headquarters monitored this. By 1943, specialised traffic for the invasion and other war efforts had a code of priorities, with actual code names being applied as the traffic was moved. We knew traffic which was required for the proposed invasion landings by its code 'Overlord', and other build-ups and schedules had to be revised frequently to enable Control and other staff to identify and urge forward the traffic.

I worked on this for about nine months, then I was moved back to headquarters to take over a small section under Fred Margetts dealing with transits and generally watching and correcting as far as possible departures from the plan. This was important to me personally as it placed me in a 'Special class', entitling me to first class travel for myself and my wife. It also brought me back into headquarters work, with the need to think to a wider horizon, to meet with other railway headquarters staff, and to get an insight into other North Eastern Districts' problems. In fact, as a result of problems arising with local freight train working to docks, collieries, steel firms, etc, and the bonus schemes applying to each trip, very soon Lance Ibbotson, Trains Assistant to the Superintendent, sent me off for a year with a team of three to examine on the spot every local working (pick-ups, mineral trains, dock trips, the lot) from Berwick to Doncaster. Economies had to be found as there was evidence of waste, and the whole schedule had to be improved. Our objective was to reduce engine hours (and thus the number of engines) in local traffic working, achieve quicker clearance of running lines and improvement in clearance times in factory sidings, and this often resulted in improvements in transit times of goods, and quicker turn-round of wagons.

First of course, this meant making our peace with the District Office people, and then working out a plan so that we all in turn covered the selected area for any one week. We had to find lodging accommodation, not easy in those dark days, which would allow us to sleep any time in the 24 hours, since the clock imposed no limitations on what we were required to do. We fed mostly in canteens, and pretty well too. We shared the good trips and the bad trips amongst our team, listing the journeys to be examined and ultimately covering all the local working, including also yard operations. We then discussed what we had to recommend with the District Officers, the 'trains' people, who, when it was agreed, had the job of implementing this changed working. We submitted weekly reports to the headquarters freight train chief and the Trains Assistant, for his information.

It was while I was on this work – the special inquiry section – that I became conscious, as at no time previously, either as an Inspector, or controller, or senior freight train clerk, of the need for statistical evaluation. Previously, figures somehow meant a woolly measurement, but now their application to production costs for each aspect of movement meant a great deal. Each District's results, each marshalling or goods yard, each station, each train's performance, could be assessed. The movements were now real, made by men and equipment, seen as they were being done, and interpreted with a new and potent meaning. Each move in train operation meant cost to the organisation, and each statistic meant a measure of that cost when properly interpreted, and its worth in terms of 'productivity'.

My mind went back to the days when, in the Statistics Office, I was multiplying wagons by miles in the guards' journals. Now here I was living on the trains and observing the guards record their work, the enginemen's work, and that of the locomotives engaged in the work. I also saw at first hand how the difference in yard or siding layout affected the performance, and how gradients, density of traffic and its fluctuations, line occupation, weather conditions, level of achievement by men and differing locomotives and so on, made comparisons between one yard or function with another most difficult. It all pointed to the need for a thorough knowledge of these factors to interpret the figures supplied daily, and to judge where to seek improved working. It was also necessary to differentiate between what top management (ie the General Manager) needed and what was needed by each level of authority down the scale in order to monitor the responsibility of each.

The author.

The station staff at Bainton in 1923. From the left: myself, W. Branton, Station Master E. G. Welburn, and another porter signalman.

York Goods Station in 'horse and cart' days, where I started work in the autumn of 1922. Now known as the Peter Allen Building, it is part of the National Railway Museum, and was used for the Great Railway Show during 1990-91. *(National Railway Museum, York)*

The North Eastern Railway Headquarters Offices in York, completed in 1906.
(National Railway Museum, York)

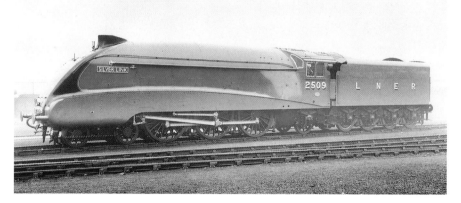

Gresley 'A4' 'Pacific' No 2509 *Silver Link*, one of four 'Silver' locomotives introduced
in September 1935 to haul the 'Silver Jubilee' streamlined express, our pride and joy on
the East Coast Main Line. *(National Railway Museum, York)*

Lowingham Sproat, LNER District Operating Superintendent at York, for whom I went to work in 1938. He was a tall man, meticulous, solid, with a deep sonorous voice.

During the Second World War I became Signalmen's Inspector for the York area, which included York Locomotive Yard signal box, at that time the largest manually operated box in the country. *(National Railway Museum, York)*

Air raids on York. Debris from part of York Station roof lies outside the Control Office in 1942 . . .

. . . and *Sir Ralph Wedgwood* destroyed by a direct hit on the locomotive shed. *(both National Railway Museum, York)*

East Coast Main Line rejuvenation: the launch of the 'Tees-Tyne' Pullman in September 1948. C. P. Hopkins (left), CRO of the NE Area, watches as author and playwright Esther McCracken performs the ceremony. I am standing between them in the background. *(Northern Echo)*

'Even the Teddy-bear? Yes, he's going to sit comfortably on this "Self-Help" Luggage Barrow at Scarborough!' The 'Hickbarrow' as seen in BR *Staff News*, June 1958.

A typical office outing in the 1950s . . .

. . . a typical office social in the 1950s . . .

. . . and a typical Regional Board Meeting in the 1950s. The Chairman of the Regional Board, T. H. Summerson, stands fifth from the left. *(British Railways)*

A meeting of the Central Transport Consultative Committee in the Board Room at Headquarters, *circa* 1956. Second on the left is E. W. Arkle, third is Lord Rusholme. First on the right is Lord Rochdale, fourth is H. A. Short, with myself to his right. Note the magnificent oval table and candelabra – now gone.

At the Railway Ball in the Assembly Rooms, 1952. Myself and Hilda on the left, with Peggy and Bernard Jessop.

Inspection Saloon No 902179 (still lettered 'LNER') behind ex-NER T. W. Worsdell 'J19' 0-6-0 No 65042 of 1886, photographed in 1960. I am standing on the platform at the extreme right.

Open forum – meeting the public at Harrogate in 1961.

Operating Conference, Windsor, April 1963. Back row, l to r: Messrs T. V. Nicholson (BRB), H. Gould (Sec'y), H. E. Roberts (SR), H. C. Sanderson (BRB), D. Bowick (ER), Morgan (WR), J. Skerrett (NER), a WR man (?), Willmot (SR). Middle row: Messrs C. Wright (BRB), R. Hider (LTE), C. Bennett (LMR), J. Sampson (LMR), J. Urquhart (ScR), J. Burge (ER), J. Galbraith (ScR). Front row: myself, and Messrs Bob Howes (LMR), R. Shervington (SR), H. Hoyle, G. Fiennes, G. Crabtree, Bill Lattimer (WR), Dick Jackson (ScR), Stuart Ward (ER).

Visit of the 'Railway Queen' to the Railway Convalescent Home at Llandudno in September 1966. L to r: myself, Matron Miss M. Moylan, SRN, Queen's Medal for Nursing, my wife, 'Railway Queen' Miss Barbara Fletcher, and Mr Pearson, Secretary of the RCH. (*M. J. Taylor*)

The Railway Convalescent Home at Dawlish – 'a superb centre'. (RCH)

Retirement, 1969. L to r: Dr Mackenzie, D. S. M. Barrie, A. W. McMurdo, I. G. MacGregor, myself, J. Sampson and H. Ormiston.

Sir Peter Parker addressing retired staff at the Friends' Meeting House, London (a fishing story?). To his right sits R. S. Goodchild, and to his left Sir Henry Johnson and myself. Also on the platform were Sidney Weighell and Tom Jenkins. *(British Railways)*

'The ruin I bought.' Stonestar in the Lake District, before (1962) and after (1966).

At the present time, no doubt highly mechanised processes by computer can produce whatever figures are required easily and quickly. Just before I retired, studies were being made of an American control system abbreviated to TOPS (Total Operating Processing System) capable of providing current detailed information on all aspects of the movement of trains, wagons, coaches and other units. It was eventually adopted by BR, and through its computer capacity it can produce the statistical as well as customer information required by management to measure performance, quickly and comprehensively.

In my day, such mysterious combinations as were necessary were derived from the following basic figures:

Section of Line	Wagon Miles		Hours		Train Miles		Wagon Miles	
	Loaded	Empty	Train	Shunting by train engines	Total	Per hour	Per train mile	Per train engine hour

Special supervision of individual express freight trains, especially relating to punctuality results, was exercised at all levels.

Passenger train statistics were mainly centred on punctuality, the main line services being individually of the highest importance, and each morning being the subject of close scrutiny at all operating levels.

We learned enormously from working so closely with the District and ground staff. Our geography and knowledge of layouts and other facilities became encyclopaedic, our acquaintance with staff was prodigious, and our stock at HQ was the 'tops'! The freight train group return, the measure of freight train performance, supported our claims, and at that time the NE figures were widely acclaimed. By the time we reached the south of the North Eastern Area we were tired and looking for a normal life. We had worked all hours in the blackout, we had struggled through snow, frost and fog, overcome awkward confrontations with war-weary people, carried on during air raids, some of which were too near to be comfortable, been away from home all week each week, bumped our jerky way in guards' vans over colliery lines, and the rest. All this led to the comment made by my able companions while walking on the edge of St Andrew's Dock, Hull, after a gruelling air raid, that a short cut out of it all would be to be thrown into the slime and fish entrails of the water below! Instead, we went to Hull Infirmary in response to an SOS and gave blood to the transfusion service!

While writing my concluding report on our activities over the previous ten months, I was asked if I would like to go to London, on the Eastern Counties side of the Southern Area of the LNER, as head of the freight trains section at Shenfield, the location of which the Liverpool Street offices had been evacuated. In view of the current bombing by 'doodlebugs', I knew that I would not want my family to go, but after a good deal of thought and consultation we agreed, as a family, that I should say 'Yes', leaving the family in York. So off I went, incurring weekend travel home, which then meant a four-hour journey time from York to King's Cross and two further hours to Shenfield – overall a six-hour journey each way. Saturday morning working was still in operation, so that cut my free time down considerably. However, there were other migrants in the London area so we clubbed together and whiled away our time in a game of poker or other card swindle on the train journeys.

This was a major change for me – a totally new geographical railway, a throbbing, vital London exactment coupled with the special requirements of the wide open spaces of East Anglia, where it seemed as though half the United States military power was stationed.

Examining the freight train statistics for my new domain, I had visions of the changes I could bring about. Fresh from my recent experience of revitalising the working in the North East, I wrote a policy paper for submission to Alec Dunbar, who was in charge of the operating function in the Eastern counties, under Eric Rostern, Operating Superintendent for the Eastern Area. There was no train bonus scheme here and, being steeped in the value of this method of working, I could see that vast improvements were possible. As an example I took the Whitemoor/March Yard to Peterborough trips, where I reckoned about a 60 per cent improvement in the cost of trainmen's time could be achieved. But I had not done my 'political' homework. The scheme was thrown out, lock, stock and barrel, because, I was told, Eric Rostern would not hear of any bonus element, and neither would Barrington Ward, the chief of Operations at the Railway Executive, who in any case would not countenance anything which was the brainchild of C.M. Jenkin Jones, General Manager of the North Eastern Area.

Without declaring too much, however, I introduced one of the potent facets of the bonus scheme. The men were advised that if they completed two trips in their shift between Whitemoor and Peterborough they could go home. They had been doing two trips with considerable overtime, and sometimes finding reasons to do only one trip. This new arrangement caught on and in consequence considerable overtime payments were saved and, what was more important, locomotives were released earlier for further work at a time when power was seriously inadequate.

I knew that there was, in general, opposition in the Eastern Area and at headquarters to freight train bonus schemes, but facts as available in the North East proved to me beyond any shadow of a doubt that productivity shot up when they were introduced and monitored (a basic need), without prejudicing safety in working. I had lived closely with their operation during the past year – in the marshalling yards, on the trains, in the colliery, steel and other private sidings, all places where time could be lost, the incentive of bonus payments worked. I had seen and heard reactions from drivers, guards, yard staff and, indeed, customers, whose sidings were involved. My Eastern Area colleagues used to say that bonus schemes were a cover-up for inadequate supervision, and a payment to the men which was not really justified because the work ought to be done in that time anyhow. Pie in the sky! With the multitude of colliery sidings and 'nooks and crannies' of the 1940s, it was impossible to have personal supervision continuously, and 'boys will be boys', whatever so-called immoral implications may be levied at the practice. Realism was somehow side-tracked in favour of a persuasive belief. One could hardly reconcile the Eastern Area thinking that a train bonus was immoral, when goods shed handling bonus payments, which they operated, were not!

Later, when I returned to York and when Arthur Dean was General Manager, he had the same approach and appointed a team, mainly from his earlier department (not from Operating!) to produce a case for the elimination of train bonus arrangements in the Hull district. He did not approve of the ingredients inherent in the scheme – and there were, in truth, some weaknesses. Apart from the fact that he appointed and instructed the team without consulting me as departmental officer concerned, he made it plain the direction in which he wanted the inquiry to go. Of course the team tried, but train bonus remained in operation and the 'flush' faded. I was not provided with the report – officially! I regret that I detect in myself some very sour grapes!

My job at Shenfield was a temporary joint appointment, operating and motive power. This merging of interests had been adopted some years earlier on the LNER, so I had to answer to the Motive Power Superintendent as well as the Operating chief. Once a week I had a session with the former, Mr L. P. Parker, who on my entry to his office sat upright in a large, well-upholstered chair, firing questions which he had obviously either previously thought out himself or had been supplied with. This austere procedure was, I was sure, adopted to establish his authority within the organisation so that no one would be under the impression that he was a junior partner. Be that as it may, one had to agree that his stance was individualistic. His approach to questioning could be somewhat menacing if there was the slightest hesitation in answering; as one of my colleagues once said of him, 'He is comparable to a Spanish inquisitor who at any moment could say to his attendant, with an autocratic gesture, "Off with his head".' On one visit to his sanctum he asked a question and threw across his desk a slide rule with the object of my working out a calculation by this method. My mathematical skills in the use of technical aids was virtually nil, and I told him so. But I said, 'I am going on holiday next week and I will give you the pleasure of testing me when I return as to my competence with a slide rule.' I proved that later. When he met my wife and I at the VE 'end of war' party, our relationship proved very happy indeed and my head remained intact!

I spent some time in the Cambridge and Norwich districts during the fruit season when train loads of soft fruits and vegetables were dispatched by rail for destinations all over the country. It was an intensive working when time was of the essence – strawberries raspberries, blackcurrants, etc, could not be delayed, so pressure had to be maintained continuously to ensure train plans based on forecast delivery could be adhered to. As anyone who worked in the Cambridge, March and Whitemoor areas will know, seasonal traffics were a feature demanding the highest possible attention. There was, too, heavy military traffic associated with the large American forces based in the Eastern counties, and frequent visits to the War Office were necessary with military transport officers to plan important movements.

The permanent holder of my temporary post, Willie Thorpe (later Deputy Chairman, British Railways Board), returned to Shenfield in November 1945 (we lodged together at Olly Frost's – renowned, and deservedly so) and I was asked to take over as Head of Passenger Trains – a lateral move. The problems in this field were much more immediate than on the freight side, especially in the London suburban areas, causing dislocation of services which resulted almost daily in reaction from the travelling public through the press and in deputations to headquarters. There was an acute shortage of manpower at Stratford, the key centre on which so many of the train movements were based. There were also shortages at other depots and frequently passenger trains were cancelled at short notice, causing considerable aggravation to passengers concerned. For the first six weeks in the job I went every evening, Monday to Friday, to Liverpool Street station, into the main signal box, and in conjunction with District and station staff made adjustments on the spot to train services. Some limited stock trains would leave Liverpool Street with 1,000 passengers on board, severely overcrowded, with passengers struggling to get on. Night after night there was heavy congestion on the platforms causing serious concern; every evening was a trial, but struggling on we would think there was an improvement until a train crew, their 'day' being long over time, would abandon their train in Stratford station. Somehow, from somewhere, a fresh set of men would be found, but meanwhile trains would be lining up behind each other. This situation was, one could say, inevitable, taking into account the war weariness of staff having to work under difficulties caused by the blackout, the 'buzz-bombs' and the fear and destruction they caused, the shortage of staff and the comparatively low wages. Even with staff recruited for work on firing locomotives there was inadequacy from lack of experience causing drivers a much more difficult task. (The young inexperienced firemen were locally referred to as 'Ovaltinies', and they would down tools at the drop of a hat!) Old coaching stock, old locomotives, and old signalling apparatus meant that only the indomitable spirit of most kept the wheels turning. I made one significant change in existing practice which assisted, and that was to prohibit the conveyance of parcels traffic on any of the suburban trains between certain hours morning and evening. This produced an immediate reaction from commercial interests, including newspapers, but we stuck to our guns and it eased the working.

The war ended while I was at Shenfield and parties were held in celebration. I look back particularly on one at Alec Dunbar's house when there were present Bill (later Sir Henry) Johnson, who became Chairman of the British Railways Board, Willie Thorpe (later Vice Chairman, BRB), Gordon Stewart (later General Manager, Scottish Region) and, of course, Alec himself (later a Member of the BRB). I contemplated moving house and explored the locality, which was most attractive, but a telephone message from York stopped me in my tracks. I was asked if I could return to York and accept the post of Head of Passenger Trains for the North Eastern at, to me, an attractive salary; and it was a position I had had my eyes on for some time. Of course I gave an affirmative answer, but Eric Rostern, in a searching discussion, pressed me to stay, and I had a long tussle over the matter. However, the advantages of returning to York won the day, and at the same time, in reviewing the pattern of life at the London end compared with York and its dales, I vowed I would not go back. Subsequently I was indeed asked to go back to London but declined, and that was that.

8.

EAST COAST MAIN LINE REJUVENATION

At the end of the war I remember looking back and contemplating on those years of emotional and physical strain tempered by the urgency and demands of doing a worthwhile job and, in fact, making a real contribution to the war effort. From concern in the early days that I may have to leave the family and join the forces as so many of my colleagues had done, through the 'phoney' war, Dunkirk and the fears of invasion and bombing, to the determination to follow Churchill when, as he put it, 'We shall not flag or fail, we shall defend our island, whatever the cost may be, we shall fight on the beaches ... on the landing grounds ... in the fields and in the streets, we shall fight in the hills; we shall never surrender'. He was inspiring, individually and collectively, and when he travelled by rail in my working area, my whole effort was at maximum, as it was with others. While experiencing the bombings we carried on with an increasingly philosophical outlook – if one's name was on the missile, so be it!

Almost all of my railway work at this time was in connection with movements related to the war effort, while my off-duty time – the fire-watching, warden duties and, most of all, Royal Observer Corps work, was still subject to that as a first priority.

Outstanding events were impressed on my mind by the job I was doing at the time. For example, on the main day of the Battle of Britain I was monitoring an important signalling renewal scheme on the main line north of York, and all of us on the spot kept in touch through wireless announcements giving the score of German planes shot down, devilishly relishing each success! It was a very encouraging turn of events and an example of the way in which we followed the realities of the war, buoyed up, again, by Churchill's humour. 'When I warned [the French] that Britain would fight on alone whatever they did, their Generals told their Prime Minister and his divided Cabinet: "In three weeks England will have her neck rung like a chicken." Some chicken! Some neck!'

My responsibilities back in York were chiefly operating, but the post was joint with the Passenger Manager and the Locomotive Running Superintendent, both of whom also wanted their pound of flesh. From all quarters there were demands for a better passenger train service following the deprivations of wartime. Local services, main line services and general amenities called for more commercial recognition – better performance on the line, improved standards of coaching stock design and utilisation, and better diagramming and use of locomotives, especially on the main East Coast line and cross country services. The whole edifice required revitalising, with imagination and, more to the point, with an injection of capital expenditure. Trains of 15 and 16 vehicles (sometimes more) were operating regularly over the East Coast Main Line with a journey time from King's Cross to York of 4 hours. Signalling was cumbersome, and consequently line occupation suffered, while branch line passenger trains and local freight 'pick-ups' were taking up vital movements at busy junctions. All this, and more, required tackling. The timetable, diagramming and coaching stock sections, all within their 'depleted by war' constraints, had to pull out every stop. I lived with my opposite numbers in other Regions almost under one roof – somewhere between Edinburgh and King's Cross, or Derby, Manchester and Crewe, working up schemes – then by what might be termed 'the horse and cart' methods! There were no computers or mechanical aids whatsoever! Fortunately, my immediate chief, Bob (later Sir Robert) Lawrence, left me to it – more or less!

The policies promulgated, and the subsequent authorisation of what the East Coast timetable between London and Edinburgh should contain, was in the hands of the chief officers of the operating and passenger commercial functions in the three areas of the LNER: for the Southern Area, Messrs Rostern and Dandridge, for the North Eastern, Messrs Rutter and Burgoyne, and for the Scottish, Messrs Sayers and Marr. A sub-committee composed of Hoyle, Hick and Nicholson, with their respective timetable staffs, prepared the schedules, including their ideas within the policies laid down, and submitted them twice yearly to meetings with the senior officers at one of the railway hotels, the Great Northern, the Royal Station or the North British, each Area taking the chair and thus the initiative in rotation. Each meeting demanded a full day's work and while we at our level tried to present a unified front, there were many occasions when wordy arguments amongst the senior officers livened up the proceedings. Policy was coloured by the practices and mentality of wartime working, when additional calls had been conceded and more extravagant timings and station allowances had been accepted for what were now to be our prestige trains – the 'what we have, we hold' syndrome! Having agreed future policy, the train schedule for the next timetable was considered – speeds, station calls, the standard of service at stations and on the trains, catering, sleeping car facilities, new fast services and the naming of prestige trains.

I spent a lot of time planning and negotiating all that was required for the original 'Tees-Tyne' Pullman from Newcastle to King's Cross and return. In conjunction with the Pullman Car Co, the Southern Area at Gerrards Cross and the Railway Executive representatives, I prepared a paper and timing schedule for eventual approval by all concerned, and was present at the train's inaugural run on 27 September 1948. In addition to some chief officers of the North Eastern Area and the Pullman Car Co, there were civic dignitaries from Newcastle, Gateshead,

Sunderland and Darlington at Newcastle Central station to give the new luxury train an official send-off. It was a follow-up in Pullman terms to the 'South Yorkshireman', the 'Yorkshire Pullman' and the 'Queen of Scots'. Before the train left, Mr C.P. Hopkins, the CRO of the NE Area, invited Esther McCracken, the well-known author, playwright and broadcaster, to perform the ceremony. This she did by anointing the headboard of 'A1' Class No 60115, then the newest type of 'Pacific'.

There was considerable discussion concerning the name this train should carry, the 'Tyne-Tees Pullman' being the most popular. However, there was a shipping company bearing this name, as well as other concerns, so it was eventually agreed to put the word 'Tees' first, much to the approval of important steel and chemical customers located on Tees-side who used the train from and to Darlington. Years of attrition on the Pullman policy eventually saw the withdrawal of the service, but I was delighted when the train was reinstated recently.

One might ask what were the implications of all this travelling to seek cohesion in producing a timetable. As mentioned, our committee met in railway hotels and consequently we were away from home very frequently. It was fortunate that we were accommodated and given excellent meeting room facilities in what were regarded as 'our' hotels. We were served coffee and lunch on the spot, so saving time, and if we managed to be free in the evening we just had to sort out our own entertainment. In Edinburgh, for instance, we were invariably invited to Freddie Margett's house at Corstorphine and joined in the noble game of poker. Freddie was the Assistant Operating Superintendent, under H. G. Sayers, of the Scottish Region of the LNER. The gathering would include Freddie, Frank Batty, Reg Rose, Cliff Birch, Harold Hoyle, Arthur Middleton and myself. All-night sessions were not unknown, but one night, finishing our game at about 4 am, we decided to walk back to the North British – some 3 or 4 miles. One of our party, who shall be nameless, and who was in lodgings, found on reaching his lodgings that he had forgotten his key and was locked out. He had to spend the rest of the night in his office, while we meanwhile disappeared into the hotel!

But that was not the end of the story. We made a somewhat late rising to find that all our shoes (which in those days were placed outside the bedroom door in the corridor to be cleaned) had been changed around by some bright spark. Single shoes were found upstairs on another floor, others were at the far end of the corridor! Chaos! But it was all sorted out in the end.

I must tell of another event at the North British. The bedroom doors were recessed off the landing two at a time, one door to the right and one to the left. Returning to my room one night, instead of inserting the key in the right-hand door I inadvertently turned left. The key fitted the door, I opened it and was flabbergasted to see, sitting up in bed and reading a book, a most attractive girl! What could I say or do? The penny dropped – I apologised, turned and fled. She didn't scream. No sequel. She just eyed me warily at breakfast the next morning. And that is a true story!

Speaking of railway hotels, I cannot think what we would have done without them during the war and the immediate post-war years. The very nature of our job, so involved with inter-regional workings and management issues, demanded discussion between responsible officers. There were no computers, fax machines, or the modern communications equipment of today. The facilities at the Royal Station Hotel at York in providing meeting rooms and meals for headquarters senior staff was a godsend, the management there bending over backwards to see that we were properly catered for. Still, the railway General Manager represented 'the boss'. The hotels management in any case felt that they were part of the railway family, and of course their staff had travel facilities on the trains. Our York senior officers' mess was located on the first floor of the hotel and we got to know the staff well. During the period of the rehabilitation of train services, therefore, we had, in fairness to people in the Regions concerned, to take turns in choosing a venue for meetings. So we only had to ask our secretary to book the necessary accommodation and all was well.

As we have seen, the Edinburgh meetings were invariably held in the North British adjacent to Waverley Station. London meetings were often at the Great Northern at King's Cross, but, depending on the Regions involved, we also sampled the Great Eastern at Liverpool Street, the Euston Hotel at Euston, the Great Western Royal Hotel at Paddington, and many others. Within the North Eastern region, apart from the Royal Station Hotel at York already referred to, we used the Royal Station Hotel at Hull, the Queens at Leeds, the Zetland at Saltburn, the Grand at West Hartlepool and the Royal Station at Newcastle.

Refreshment rooms were available at all the larger stations, and they were part of the railway organisation; together with the hotels, they at different times victualled the inspection saloons used by senior and District officers.

This close association between the railway function and the catering side was accepted as the norm – a natural growth from the days when their services were an integral part of rail travel. In the 1940s and 1950s, who would have believed that this side of the business would one day no longer be part and parcel of the industry. But that day dawned after I retired, and the glories of those prestige hotels have now faded into a memory.

Cross country services over the Pennines and those from the North East to the South West were the Cinderella of main line services despite many efforts to improve them and give them attention comparable to that received by the East Coast Main Line. We spent many hours with our colleagues from Derby, Crewe and Manchester (ie the Midland, London & North Western, and Lancashire & Yorkshire spheres of interest). I remember meetings at Carlisle, Derby, Crewe and Chinley, all representatives trying to secure a 'new look' cross country timetable, but in the event failing to achieve it. Inborn prejudices, physical limitations over the running lines (curves, colliery workings, capacity and availability of loco-motives, demarcations of trainsmen's working knowledge and agreements), and a whole host of reasons were advanced for not doing what was needed. Though it was appreciated that the traffic flows were not comparable with those of the East Coast, it was nevertheless a disappointing aspect of my sojourn in that job. It might have been the lack of interest by the senior officers concerned, or the old constituent companies' jealousies still persisting, with concentration centred on the most profitable lines which more quickly reflected their action!

While I was deep in the throes of competing for status trains on the LNER, improving speeds, reporting on coaching stock design and other post-war requirements, a major event occurred. On 1 January 1948, nationalisation took place and produced 'British Railways'. Strangely, this did not make much impression on me and did not change in any way my outlook towards my work. I contended that 'the railway' was my employer, and my effort, my aims and my drive to make a proper contribution at all times motivated me – not whether the system belonged to private or public bodies – and that is how many of my contemporaries felt. In the event, we found that being one comprehensive whole nevertheless facilitated working and planning, and since then it has developed over more than 40 years into a very intricate and complicated operation, between many interdependent and interlacing functions. I feel that a return to privatisation involving a number of independent owners would lead to accountability problems, inter-planning and operational disputes, (worse than the old 'penetrating lines'!) and internecine commercial warfare, since all owners, at some stage or other, would be using much common-user staff and hardware. Traffic conditions and practices today are far removed from those of 1948, and the situations cannot be compared with the 'service' motive of those days and the 'profit' motive of today.

One could say, however, that if the whole of BR went to one body with a single direction, the change would hardly be felt. There would, of course, be the 'Beeching' or 'Parker' influence, rather than the 'Johnson' or 'Reid'. But who would be the 'Great' arbiter?

Publishing the timetable for public use, which was normally done twice a year (Summer and Winter – at one time an additional Spring issue was also prepared) demanded target dates for the preparation and agreement of each stage. Each area of the LNER and each section of other lines had its own timetable, the contents of which had been agreed inter-regionally, and such items as date of operation, type of print to be used, national advertising features and certain other all-line considerations were all predetermined in conjunction with, after nationalisation, the Railway Executive. It was quite a procedure, interchanging timings for each other's timetables; and then, of course, there were Bradshaw and other privately published timetables which, by request, had to be catered for. Bradshaw included the timings and other relative information for all railways in the country, as well as connection by domestic sea links. It was a massive fount of information, issued monthly.

A close working relationship with the printers was necessary and it was a sad time while I was in the section when, on instruction from the Railway Executive, we had to take the work away from Chorley and Pickersgill of Leeds and place it with McCorquodale's. The 'Gill Sans' type was also abandoned, which I regretted. The regular printers who did the work were experts and drew attention many times to odds and ends which required correction – they were splendid timetable clerks! Our own staff now had to spend time away from home with the printers passing the final manuscript when it was transferred from Leeds, whereas a day trip to C&P had been no problem. Despite all our pre-planning, we rarely had the timetables on the stations' booking desks for the start of the new book. Three or four days to two weeks late caused the usual row and we were in trouble. As soon as it was received, however, the storm abated and we were already preparing for the next edition! We do not seem to be getting any better in 1991!

During my time as head of timetable section we had to work in close relationship with the advertising department who published special features on each issue of the timetable. Many new ideas were featured, especially one encouraging passengers to take an interest from their seat looking through the carriage window. One such document, not published by the railway but by the author, Mr S.N. Pike MBE, aroused considerable interest. It was for those travellers between King's Cross and Edinburgh over the East Coast Main Line, and was entitled *Mile by Mile on the LNER* and gave a most fascinating picture of the geographical and operating features visible from the train as it sped along the track. I reproduce an extract from this excellent brochure in Appendix C covering the line within the North Eastern area in which I had so much interest.

9.

THE HOLY OF HOLIES

After just over four years in the very interesting post of Head of Passenger Trains during the rehabilitation of post-war services, a job I revelled in and looked forward to on Monday mornings when I knew some creative work awaited me, I was approached by Bernard Jessop, Assistant Regional Officer, NE Region, to see if I would be interested in taking a post in the Chief Regional Officer's office as head of General Section. This section dealt with traffic matters in the Region at top level, and the only doubt I had was that I might get isolated from what I always regarded as 'real' railway working, and find difficulty in getting back. However, after further discussion with 'B.X.J.,' and with Mr H. A. Short, Chief Regional Officer, I was appointed in April 1951.

No sooner had I arrived than an urgent call from the British Transport Commission, then the top level of management of railways in the country, that each Region must re-orientate its Civil Defence organisation and appoint a regional Civil Defence Officer. Some Regions appointed a full-time officer, but not so the North Eastern, and I was designated to undertake the duties, now to be radically increased, along with my other work. I knew nothing whatsoever about the subject, but there it was, and I had to get on with it, bearing in mind that General Slim (of Burma fame) was the Board member responsible, and there would be frequent contact with his staff, and he himself on occasion. The first thing I did was to appoint a good assistant, Wilf Richardson, full time, who would do all the work! At least that was the idea, but soon I was at Sunningdale on a training course learning about 'röntgens', chemical attacks, detectors of various kinds, and all the paraphernalia and horrible potential of things past, things present, and things to come in a new brand of warfare.

The potential effect on rail transport was, of course, the main source of our study, and to review our progress General Slim spent part of the concluding day with us, when it was made evident that the subject had to be taken very seriously. The arrangements for an emergency had to be consistent throughout the railway system, and they had to be known and understood, so after the initial baptism in this extra-mural work, I was able to use my Civil Defence assistant to the full, in order to leave

76

me free for my 'proper' job. Nevertheless the Civil Defence work went on for a number of years and I had to attend committee meetings with the BTC chairman of Civil Defence matters acting on behalf of General Slim whose great personality inspired us.

But first and foremost, my duties were concerned with traffic policies, helping to form them or developing ideas in the pipeline. Much of this came to me from the Chief Regional Officer who asked for a memo on subjects up for discussion at the Railway Executive. I had to draw up agendas for his meetings with his Regional Officers, which he called every three months when all attended, and more frequently when he saw selected officers. I then prepared papers dealing with items on the agenda and produced the draft minutes after each meeting (the same day) for his approval. These meetings often called for action which I had to initiate and later pursue, and undoubtedly my experience in various capacities at lower levels, and with practical knowledge to boot, stood me in good stead. I had splendid help on the way. One Bob Reid (recently Chairman, BRB), Myles Herbert (later Chief Passenger Manager, LMR) and Lloyd Gray-Jones (later Freight Business Manager, SR) came to me at different times in those early days, all of immense assistance.

In this post-war demand for progress, these full departmental meetings held by the CRO gave the various departmental officers the opportunity through their work measurement figures to report on developments, and to generate new moves in what inevitably was a 'wide-open field'. It could be quite stimulating though as, creeping into the whole concept of railway economics, the cost factor began to compete with what had so long been in domination – the service factor. I remember the contributions made by E. W. Arkle, designated Commercial Officer, in charge of the traffic side, who in masterly fashion outlined over a very wide field 'the state of the nation'. All North Eastern officers were domiciled in York except the Chief Mechanical Engineer, Carriage and Wagon Engineer, Accountant, Continental Traffic Manager, Road Motor Engineer, Store Superintendent and Treasurer, such officers having joint responsibility with the Eastern Region. In addition, E. W. Rostern was Operating Superintendent of the Eastern and North Eastern Regions, the most senior post under him being occupied by A. P. Hunter, designated Divisional Operating Superintendent.

In those early days of nationalisation, there was a strange relationship between operating Regions known as 'penetrating lines', which meant that some Regions were responsible for running into other Regions' geographical territories, operating only, and the officer supervising this had to report to the Chief Regional Officer of that 'penetrated' Region – a most complicated organisation. Charles Whitworth of the Eastern Region and myself were eventually delegated to draw up a plan, ultimately successful, to eliminate this arrangement between the ER and the NER, geographical boundaries determining the sphere of operating and regional responsibilities.

The meetings with departmental officers took place in the splendid North Eastern Railway Board Room, round that outsize oval table, under two large and attractive candelabra, with the eyes of bygone railway giants gazing down from their magnificent gilt-framed portraits. That historic table and the candelabra have gone – some of the 'family silver' has been sold!

It was shortly after arriving in the office that I was asked to be a trustee of the Railway Convalescent Homes, a railway charity in which I had shown some interest. I became specially identified with a beautiful home at Ilkley which I visited regularly at weekends, reporting periodically to a board of trustees. Later I became visiting trustee for the Llandudno centre, a superbly positioned home overlooking the Conway estuary and Snowdonia. I have been proud to be associated with the organisation for nearly 40 years and continue that interest as a Vice President. As with many charities, the RCH has had its ups and downs, but its faithful rank and file volunteers have kept this worthwhile effort going and I sincerely wish it well. I will later comment further on this subject.

One of the accompanying photographs shows the 'Railway Queen' visiting the Railway Convalescent Home at Llandudno, known as 'the Old Abbey' after the ruins of an old abbey in its grounds. The charming ceremony of crowning the daughter of a railway family, initiated and directed by the National Union of Railwaymen and supported by other rail unions and by the railway administration and staff generally, was an annual event drawing a large attendance at Trafford Park, Manchester. The lucky young lady then had the honour of visiting various places of railway interest throughout the following year where she was acclaimed and the event celebrated, usually on a Saturday when more staff were free to entertain her. One such occasion is recorded in the photograph, and below is an extract from *Railnews* of October 1966, which described the event:

BARBARA VISITS LLANDUDNO CONVALESCENT HOME

Britain's railway queen, Miss Barbara Fletcher, was recently the invited guest of the railway convalescent fund to see the work being done to care for patients recovering from sickness at the Old Abbey Home at Llandudno. A reception party comprising the matron, Miss M. A. Moylan, SRN, Dr and Mrs Wynn-Hughes, medical officer, and Mr and Mrs F. L. Hick, trustee of the homes, welcomed Miss Fletcher and expressed the opinion that she would like what they had to show her.

After talking to the patients, Miss Fletcher was taken on a tour of the buildings and grounds, which she could only describe as 'luxurious' and, indeed, she found that that was the opinion of those who were fortunate enough to have such a residence to recover from illness, and it was a unanimously expressed opinion that after only a few days in such comfortable and convivial surroundings, the ladies were feeling very much better.

Before leaving the home, Miss Fletcher received a brooch from Mr F. L. Hick which had been made specially for the Railway Queen and bore the insignia of all the railway convalescent homes.

It was a lovely idea giving joy to many people, especially children, and creating a lively, warm relationship on those occasions of mutual interest. Many senior officers attended the crowning ceremony and I for one enjoyed the event and the atmosphere it engendered.

This was the British Transport Commission era and the theory of a nationally integrated transport system was abroad – it was expected that all forms of transport would be drawn together and work together, and all would belong to a happy family. People from road transport were brought into railway service and vice versa, such moves being greeted as a major indication of co-operation under the auspices of the BTC, whereas in reality it was a matter of 'window dressing' since there was a great reluctance to take our former competitors into our confidence, and vice versa. In the passenger, freight and parcels fields we were being asked to meet top people from the various organisations, and I became involved in a number of committees, meeting non-railway operators and discussing what to do next. With the best will in the world, and there was plenty of good will and friendship, we were all looking over each other's shoulders, wondering who was poaching what! It was 'pie in the sky', together with that later all-star example of the 'freightliner', a great railway concept and in railway ownership later taken over by Sir Reginald Wilson's road organisation, then returned to the railways with a doubtful future.

Sir Brian Robertson, Chairman of the BTC, made a tour of the North East and I accompanied the CRO (or was he now Chief Regional Manager?*) when various aspects of modernisation were discussed and in particular electrification of the East Coast Main Line. In fact, as part of the 'Modernisation Plan' of 1954, the Eastern and North Eastern were to submit a report setting out the implications of electrifying the East Coast line to Leeds and Newcastle with possible extensions to Hull and Tees-side. I was delegated to represent the North Eastern and John Bonham Carter the Eastern. It was a formidable job, collecting the data for all aspects of the project, engineering, commercial, operating with motive power, signalling, the effect on outside interests, and so on. John took the initiative, prepared the finished report and presented it to Sir Brian Robertson and his Board at a meeting at Liverpool Street, with myself available for any points to answer re the North Eastern. After satisfying the Chairman and Board, the scheme was accepted, but unfortunately was not finally approved for implementation. What a great step forward that would have been, at the exceptionally low cost of the 'fifties – a golden opportunity missed.

Following the Transport Act of 1947, the Central Transport Consultative Committee sought the constitution of Area Transport Users' Consultative Committees, and the first of these affecting the North Eastern was based in Newcastle covering the geographical area from Northallerton to Berwick. I was asked to organise the arrangements for introducing the committee hearings and to act as its first Secretary, the cost of such meetings to be borne by the railway.

*The Chief Regional Officer of 1953 became Chief Regional Manager in 1954 and General Manager in 1955. In 1952 my position was redesignated Assistant to CRO (General), later to be amended to Assistant to General Manager (General).

The first Chairman was Sir Mark Hodgson, from Labour ranks and a former President of the Confederation of Engineering and Shipbuilding Unions. He was a wise adjudicator and knew so well how to handle difficult situations, and was seen by his TUCC committee, by the public and by the railways as a fair assessor and decision-maker. I worked frequently and happily with him. He readily gave 'tips' in the art of negotiation and openly revealed the techniques and tactics inherent in his previous occupation; he was a grand old man who later became a member of the North Eastern Board. His main TUCC task for some years was dealing with the closure of branch lines, which meant many deputations from country areas and many and varied personalities making the saving of the railway line their main object in life. He and Mr Short invited the Central Transport Consultative Committee to York where they enthused at being able to sit round that oval table in the majestic Board Room in the headquarter offices, and posed to have their photographs taken on this exceptional outing.

In 1951 an 'all line' enquiry was started into the possibilities of introducing lightweight diesel multiple rail units into this country. The Ulster railways had operated them successfully and demonstrated their operating and commercial values. I was asked to represent the North Eastern Region and to prepare a scheme for consideration by the committee along with proposals from the Western, Eastern, London Midland and Scottish Regions, the Southern being excluded because of its electrified services. In discussions with colleagues in the operating and commercial departments, a scheme was drawn up to operate the units on a shuttle service between Leeds and Bradford with extensions to Harrogate, an area which seemed to us as being the most suitable and with the best potential in the Region.

The operation of such a fleet would mean a major change in railway performance – the change in traction with all its ramifications in servicing and maintenance, timing implications and all the practical issues which would be involved, and, not least of all, the reaction of trainmen and other staff whose support we were anxious to obtain. It was necessary to determine the standards of accommodation, capacities, decor, robustness, frequency of service etc, etc. The exercise was not made easier by the fact that the lines between Leeds and Bradford were still operated as a 'penetrating' line, with the operating responsibility located in London (Eastern Region). Also, unfortunately, the 'steam' officers were against the introduction of diesel traction and verbally objected to my involvement in the preparation of the scheme. Furthermore, they worked on the CRO against the introduction of diesel multiple units (DMUs) in the North Eastern Region.

However, I was eventually instructed by the CRO and pressed the case for introduction through the BR central staff. In due course I was called to London, the BTC requiring a firm proposition from the 'all line' committee as to where the first DMU scheme should operate. Present at the meeting were Mr C. K. Bird (CRO, Eastern), Mr J. Ness (CRO, Scotland), Mr G. Bowles (Asst CRO, Western), Mr S. Gould (Operating Officer, London Midland) and myself. The North Eastern scheme found favour as the major proposition, but I did wonder if that was because of hostility to diesel in the other Regions. Then came the bidding for units and again I went all out, quite outside my authority, for the maximum, and was allocated the number required for my scheme. With the full fleet in the bag, I made my way to York full of trepidation, with visions of the reaction from chief officers and the boss. However, I saw Mr Short immediately the following morning and, following various consultations, he gave his approval. The next thing was to overcome the further dissent in the Operating and Motive Power departments which took some time, but I must give A. P. Hunter (Operating Superintendent) credit in that he rang me up specially after the units had been in operation for some time, conceding that there were considerable benefits in the new form of working, and he now supported the scheme without reservation.

I was surprised to learn at a later date that during the preparation of the scheme, Mr Short had indicated to the BTC that he wished to withdraw the North Eastern from participation in the plan, but had been firmly told by the BTC to proceed. Although I was handling the matter in York, I neither heard nor saw any indication of that incident. Evidently it was thought wise to keep me out of it!

The day the working was introduced I went early morning over to Leeds. As I watched the commuters coming in from Bradford and other stations by their new form of transport, and noted with great satisfaction the complimentary remarks from our customers and the broad smiles from a reinvigorated staff, I felt very proud. Morale shot up throughout the area affected. Rightly or wrongly, I regarded this as 'my' scheme, not as the originator of the idea, which I had understood came from a Board Member, Mr Pope, but in its build-up and application, just as Freddie Margetts referred to the freight trains he developed in the NER as 'my' trains. And as it was the first major project with new lightweight DMUs in the country, all eyes were on it, and considerable interest shown. In one sense it was unfortunate that the trains proved so popular, as the weight of passengers in the coaches caused the undercarriages to bend and cause difficulty in closing the doors!

In short, the scheme was a success and became the forerunner of DMU conversion on branch lines throughout the country. The GM got the CBE, I got a rise in salary and was labelled locally as the 'diesel king' (until I surrendered the crown to George Jones of the Operating department who progressed dieselisation by DMUs in the NER), while the railways of Britain got a new dimension to their passenger profile. It was with great satisfaction that I heard in 1990 that the line between Leeds and Bradford is to be electrified. The DMUs saved it from extinction.

The wide-scale introduction of DMUs throughout the country is a story of its own. It saved many branch lines from closure, and secondary lines too, but still to the 'steam' railwayman and to many members of the public interested in railways, DMUs are dowdy, lack romance, animation, vitality and life! A pity!

Associated Humber Lines, a small shipping company based on Hull and Goole and owned privately by the railways, was placed under the chairmanship of Mr Short, who had previously been closely involved in shipping and docks at Southampton. He took a great interest in the rehabilitation of the company, whose ships had to be replaced. A modernisation plan had to be prepared and I was required to undertake some secretarial work for the provision of new ships and the re-invigoration of services to and from continental and Scandinavian ports. I was invited to Rotterdam, Amsterdam, Antwerp, Hamburg and Copenhagen to observe the working there and to meet some of the main forwarding agents, and sample some of the shipping hazards of the North Sea. However, as a sailor I was an abject failure. I only had to set foot on a ship to turn green and take immediately to my bunk. It was a series of wasted opportunities! The captain's table, on these occasions, always had a vacant seat.

During this rehabilitation period, there were many meeting in Hull with the current General Manager of the AHL and his technical advisers to discuss the implications of a large capital outlay and the potential generation of new traffic. The ships were to be built by Austin and Pickersgill of Sunderland, and were all to be named after Abbeys in Yorkshire. My wife and I went to two launchings, an experience we appreciated. This variation to my job gave my designated sub-title 'General' some significance!

We had a strong Lecture and Debating Society organisation in the North East, the history of which dated from 1904 when the York society was formed. Each District fielded a team which during the winter months discussed many and varied subjects, initiated by local committees formed of District Officers and staff, the whole idea being strongly supported by top management. The District societies were drawn together by a body known as the NE Area Federation of Lecture and Debating Societies which had a separate composition of officers (mainly top managers with a sprinkling of representatives from the Districts) and which had a programme of its own, visiting Districts in turn and usually debating matters of current significance. These meetings were important as a means of communicating new ideas or in seeking to create fresh thinking. Both District and Federation societies ran essay competitions each winter on open subjects, and it was the ambition of many young people to win the prizes offered. The Federation prize-giving was a popular annual event, much publicised in the railway staff magazine, and it was combined with an important paper with subsequent discussion, so drawing maximum attendance. So popular were these annual events that management approved the running of a special train from Hull to York or Darlington to enable staff to attend, the current ordinary passenger service not permitting the return journey late in the evening. My membership card for 1931-32 is reproduced here as an item of interest.

It was a Federation meeting at which I publicly presented the case for DMUs in the Region. The main hall of the Railway Institute in York was full and standing. Every square foot in the hall was taken and there was a great sense of anticipation. I had slides to support my story by which I was determined to convince the many, many steam fans of the virtues of the scheme which had been prepared. I put all I could into the presentation, and the debate which followed was fast and furious. Someone dared to say it would destroy the local bus service and deprive the public, to which I replied, 'Good – I couldn't care less.' Loud applause! A great moment.

The press were present and extracts from my paper formed the block-print

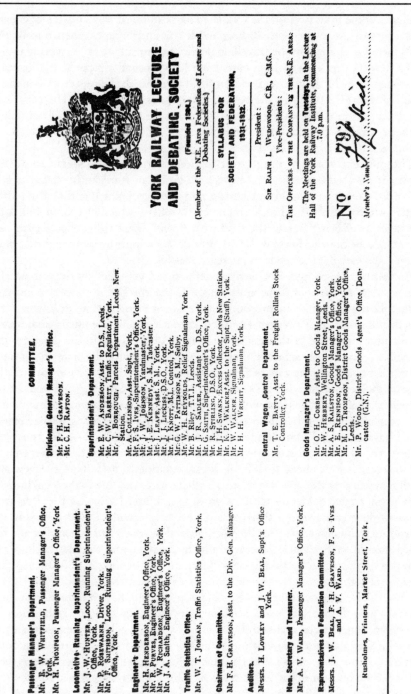

headlines of the front page of *The Yorkshire Post* next day. It was a matter, of course, of special interest to the West Riding, and it was a thrilling experience to be the harbinger of such news to the travelling public, and equally to be conveying to the staff a new concept with such promise. Later I gave a similar paper to the Institute of Transport in Newcastle and was awarded the British Transport Commission award of the year (1956) for the best paper on an original subject. The paper was printed in full in the Institute Journal and illustrates the prospect of diesel railcar operation in the North East as at September 1956. It is reproduced as Appendix A to this book.

The concept was a turning point in the transition from steam to diesel, constituting a vital component in the evolution of rural and provincial rail networks. Perhaps it would not be too immodest to point out that the North Eastern was first in this field with a major DMU scheme which succeeded, following the example of being first in the field with steam! Admittedly, experiments had been made before the Second World War on some railways with railcars, both steam and diesel, but they had not proved successful.

As will be appreciated, this development spread very quickly throughout the system once its virtues had been established, and the DMU concept continues today. The big change in present-day circumstances is that, following the introduction of PTE (Passenger Transport Executives) in large urban areas, many local authorities share in the cost of running and have a say in the design of the timetable – and rightly so, since they in most case press for the train to continue against economic circumstances. The amazing thing is that in some parts of the country the performance is not as good as in those early days, and one would have thought that after all this time, with experience and advanced technical know-how, the combined forces of those responsible for providing and designing the equipment could have produced something better than revealed in the fiasco in the West Riding (yes – I still use this descriptive term) where recent results have been grim.

However, to look ahead to 1991 it is very exciting to read about the new and ambitious plans for this area which are designed to give new life to the local lines on a five-year target. Evidently traffic is growing fast, and I visualise the 'Regional' network developing into a thriving and successful concern, and reversing the downward trend of recent years. So much depends on adequate investment and the positive outlook. 'Reshaping', the word first used with regard to railways almost 40 years ago, appears to be taking on a different and healing significance – new stations, restoring train service facilities, electrification. I wish it well!

Those Debating Society meetings could also be wounding to some. In the early 1960s, Philip Shirley, a Board Member, elected to talk to our Federation on passenger train services, and with his 'Austrylian swashbuckling' approach, he tore apart (as was his wont) the existing main line and local ideas on train planning. Naturally those of us who had spent much of our working days developing these services from a wartime low, felt somewhat ruffled, but were prepared to accept so much. When, however, he came to deride those who year after year timed the 'Flying Scotsman' to leave King's Cross at 10 am getting into Edinburgh too late for afternoon business meetings, I sat up and took notice! I was on the spot, so when question time came I couldn't wait to have a go. The 'Flying Scotsman' had left King's Cross at 10 am since 1865, nearly 100 years ago at the time of discussion. It was the premier prestige train on the railways of Britain, was known internationally, and its departure time was part of its attraction. It was then the most profitable train running on British Railways, it had a high standard of performance, it was the pride and joy of ex-LNER staff, and part of the morale-boosting element on East Coast working. To change its departure time would deprive it of its glamour and appeal. Apart from all that, there already was a train leaving King's Cross at 8 am getting passengers into Edinburgh in time for an afternoon meeting. Had that been overlooked? And so on and so forth! I knew from that moment I would be classified as 'dead wood', but someone had to demonstrate the pride in something 'traditional'. And I still think I was right! I regret to say the speaker did not reply directly. He had dropped a 'clanger'!

It is sad in my opinion that someone has since amended the King's Cross departure time of the 'Flying Scotsman' to 10.30 am. Sacrilege! There ought to have been a preservation order on such a hereditary symbol! But even then, although it is referred to in the timetable as the 'Flying Scotsman', the train itself does not carry a nameboard telling the outside world that it is the 'Flying Scotsman'. Locomotives can be named and carry a nameplate – but there is no such distinction for trains. Something the public love is to talk in terms of 'I wish to travel, or have travelled, on the so and so', and in this day and age of the train, naming would be an absolute winner!

Meanwhile, I had often wondered what could be done to assist passengers with their luggage, as it was impossible on crowded platforms in summer to provide staff to cover all requirements. I therefore conceived the idea of 'self-help' barrows which the passenger could use, light in weight and easily handled. With the help of a friendly contractor, a barrow was produced to my design based on rather similar lines to the farming pattern of a sack barrow. Skilfully balanced it could be handled with a minimum of effort, and was provided with hooks for handbags, umbrellas, dog leashes and other impedimenta. I had it brought to the office and at a Board Meeting with Mr T.H. Summerson in the chair, Mr Priestman, another Board Member (North Eastern) and chief of an engineering firm, presented my barrow for inspection! They christened it the 'Hickbarrow', and after I had commented on its potential, they agreed to its introduction on an experimental basis at Scarborough, where it would help to cope with the heavy holiday traffic and where there were insufficient porters to help with heavy luggage. The experiment proved so popular in 1958 that the barrows were supplied to Leeds Central, Bradford Forster Square, South Shields, Darlington, Whitby, Withersea and Hornsea in time for the holiday rush. Later the barrows were adopted in other parts of the country, despite some objections from the staff, and they survived until the new concept of passenger trolleys was introduced. I often wonder where the originals went to – I haven't seen one in the National Railway Museum! An extract from *Staff News*, North Eastern Region, of June 1958 is reproduced overleaf.

Oh! Mr. Porter. What shall I do?— Just take a "Self-Help" Luggage Barrow, And carry enough for two!

Pardon this parody on the old music hall song. Of course, we all know that when a porter is around, he will always step quickly forward to relieve the overburdened traveller of his luggage !

But in this, the really revenue-earning time of the year, when holidaymakers are pouring into inland stations to travel by train to the coast, and pouring out of the carriages at the other end to reach their seaside hotels and boarding houses, there just aren't enough human porters to go round.

So, last summer, the North Eastern Region provided a new and handy type of "Self-help" luggage barrow at Scarborough Central Station for the convenience of holidaymakers travelling with heavy luggage.

The experiment proved so popular this year, that new " Self-help " barrows have already been supplied to Leeds Central, Bradford Forster Square, South Shields, Darlington, Whitby, Withernsea and Hornsea in time for the holiday rush.

Similar to a golfer's caddy car, the "Self-help" luggage barrow is light in weight and of modern design. It weighs only 37 lbs., but has a carrying capacity of 8½ cwts. So skilfully balanced that it can be handled with a minimum of effort, the "Self-help" luggage barrow has hooks for handbags, umbrellas, dog leashes and the various impedimenta which normally go with the holidaymaker.

Bouquets for the man who thought of the bright idea— Mr. F. L. Hick, Assistant Operating Officer, North Eastern Region !

Black edging really ought to be applied to some episodes in a recorded summary of one's experience. As, for example, when I turned down a proposition made to me for a move to Hull. Whether I was selected because I had once expressed certain views on organisation to the Institute of Transport, I do not know, but here is a piece of what I had said, taken from the Institute's Journal:

LEEDS AND DISTRICT

'Railway Organisation' was the subject of a contribution presented by Mr F. L. Hick, Graduate, at a meeting of the Society held on February 15th, 1935.

The speaker drew attention to the necessity for greater co-ordination of railway work which in most cases had hitherto been divided into departments, and suggested that on large scale systems such as the group railways there should be a wider application of the divisional system. While admitting that certain sections of work , such as construction of rolling stock and heavy repairs, financial and statistical work, control of stores, legal and publicity work – were better controlled under departmental organisation, he stressed the point that commercial, operating and locomotive running work should be amalgamated under the authority of a traffic manager, and that activities under these heads should be decentralised, local administration being in the hands of divisional officers. Two main reasons were given: firstly, it seemed but logical to place under the officer who was responsible for the movement of traffic the means of moving it, and authority over the staff engaged in the process; secondly, a higher standard of service would be assured to customers if the official responsible for securing the traffic was also responsible for its conveyance. The success of the proposed arrangement would, however, depend upon how far the activities were decentralised, how close a contact could be established between the divisional officers and the trading authority was vested in the divisional officers.

It had been agreed by the NER Board (this was in 1956/57) that an experimental appointment of a new kind should be made for the Hull area – a Divisional Manager responsible for the functions in that area and reporting direct to the General Manager, superseding the existing District organisation. I understood it to be a pilot scheme, the first testing out of a new concept in regional organisation, and that Messrs Summerson, Short and Dunbar had decided to put me in the post. Of course I was not brought into the matter until they had worked out the details and meanwhile I was moving house and making other domestic arrangements for my family which virtually tied me to York, and to looking after elderly parents. I was surprised, and faced with a dilemma.

Alec Dunbar, then Assistant General Manager for the Region, discussed the matter at length with me and I agreed to take a few days to consider all the implications. However, my nerve failed me and to the disconcertion of my chiefs I asked to be excused. I myself was dismayed that such an opportunity should be turned down – very dismayed – but I felt that to take the job, which I was told would mean moving to Hull, would result in letting down my parents and that I could not do. As a result the pilot scheme was not pursued in the NER. I do not think Dunbar ever forgave me, but there it was – my home considerations triumphed for once! Perhaps after all I was right, although I knew from my knowledge of some of my colleagues that 'flitting' paid off materially and it is noted from Prof Gourvish's history of British Railways that 'Lawrence experienced 36 changes of job and 21 changes of location, while Thorpe had 45 jobs and 35 locations'.

When Divisional Managers were eventually appointed throughout the country, I dared not apply! Instead, I showed interest in a return to my old love – the Operating department – and after the necessary preliminaries made my next move as Assistant Operating Officer, in harness again with my former chief, Lowingham Sproat.

10.

RETURN TO OPERATING

Low Sproat, who had been District Superintendent at York and Newcastle (he came from Alston, son of a policeman), was revered in his native area of Tyneside. There, staff, union representatives and colleagues, all spoke highly of him, and I was delighted to be associated with him again. His title was 'Operating Officer', but so far as one could see his duty to the railway and to the public was the safety of the line and all that operated on it, along with his departmental responsibilities which had not changed in principle (though to some extent in detail and the manner in which practices had altered) since the holders of the post had been known in different terms. From my entering the service, the head of the department has been knows as:

General Superintendent
Superintendent
Operating Superintendent
Divisional Operating Superintendent
Chief Operating Superintendent
Operating Officer
Operating Officer (1) Movements Planning Manager (2)
Movements Manager
Chief Operating Manager
Regional Operating Manager

Elsewhere, the title Superintendent of the Line was used. But, one might ask, 'What's in a name?' Is there a vital significance in whether the man who runs the show in practice has 'Officer' or 'Superintendent' or 'Manager' after his name? My simple interpretation was that if certain functions were your responsibility, then it was your job to see that they were performed efficiently and within the policies and principles laid down by management at top level. That was Mr Sproat's view too, with the emphasis on 'safety'. So I returned 'home' as it were, with rumours of reorganisation at Area or District Level taking up valuable time amongst the staff running the railway. There was talk of Area Traffic Managers, Divisional Managers and Line Managers, all of which raised for me the question of how we would be affected in supervising the operating function down to 'field' level.

The first consideration, however, was to get down to the 'nitty gritty' of the job and, apart from taking an interest in the whole of the department, I was particularly requested to monitor and assist in the preparation of new signalling schemes. There were many new projects for introducing colour light signalling and power points throughout the Region where layouts were to be altered and signal boxes dispensed with, as well as level crossing improvements, many of which involved staff adjustments. I had behind me the experience of resignalling the York area when, as a Signalman's Inspector, I had been involved in the new scheme started before the war. It had been resurrected after the war and, despite the forebodings of some, it was working satisfactorily, carrying out the work previously done by seven signal boxes, but was already out of date. In fact, signalling techniques were advancing very fast and I was closely associated with the Signal Engineer in an effort to speed the working, reduce the labour force, and improve the safety with which trains were operated.

Inevitably since retirement I have continued to try to keep informed about the spectacular development of signalling techniques, and must say how effectively this has advanced operating practices and improved efficiency in movement control. There has also been, I understand, a closer welding together of operating and signalling interests over the safety factor which is inherently a mutual problem, and modern facilities are being exploited to seal this partnership.

The increasing application of electronics into the signalling and communications functions has revolutionised the train control system by visual display units in signal boxes and Control offices, thereby assisting in the determination of priorities in running and platforming. We thought that by increasing the capacity and range of operation from one signal box covering the York area, a major step forward was being taken, which in its day it was, but to see the areas covered by present installations is indeed astonishing. Compare it with the time when many signalmen in many boxes at a busy place debated which movement should be given priority, and when the outcome was often determined by one signalman's problems without due concern for the wider picture; on top of this there was the local controller in the District office also giving his view. Now one display unit covering the whole area under one signalman automatically reveals all, and only matters of higher policy need direction from senior authority.

Back in my new job, I was drawn into developments in train working, especially on the freight side. More 'continuously braked trains' and better marshalling yard facilities were needed to give quality of service and cope adequately with the still heavy traffic on rail. There were still shortages of wagons, especially steel-carrying types, and shortages of locomotives due to the high incidence of failure or delay on the line. There were wagon and locomotive balancing problems inter-regionally which had to be rectified by morning conference, and current train working difficulties came to me rather than to the Operating Officer unless they were of major significance.

Most of all, I was involved in the development of new marshalling yards which had been decided before my arrival. These were to be at Newport (Middlesbrough), Low Fell (Gateshead) and the West Riding (at a place to be decided, but most likely Stourton). A special section of staff who were knowledgeable on freight working requirements was formed and responded direct to me. These new marshalling yards, financed as a result of the Modernisation Plan produced by the BTC, presented enormous problems in maintaining current working at the same time, especially at Newport; the replacing of freight services and the ancillary requirements had not been too well defined in the original thinking. The West Riding yard was well advanced in planning when the BTC decided against it, and the scheme was abandoned. This was to prove a right and timely decision, as things turned out later.

The development of diesel traction was proceeding apace. While in the General Manager's office I had been concerned with the plans for introduction of diesel locomotives over the East Coast Main Line in addition to DMUs on local lines and, on transfer to the Operating department I was requested to continue. I had already visited the English Electric works at Newton-le-Willows with members of the NE Area Board and the engineers involved, and had gathered the necessary facts and figures of the proposed 'Deltic'-types for the service, which would enable performance to be measured. The 'Deltic' was the first diesel locomotive in the world to house power equipment with as high a horsepower as 3,300 on a single 'Co-Co' chassis with a maximum axle loading of 18 tones – a powerful giant indeed. I therefore now had to work with Eastern and Scottish Region people in drawing up a timetable using the new locomotives. Diagrams for men and machines, maintenance schedules, loads, new works and so on had to be drawn up and put in hand. Replacing 55 steam locomotives, the fleet of 22 'Deltics', due to arrive in 1960-61, were capable of hauling heavier trains than the existing steam fleet at higher constant speeds, so it really was a major operational project which had to be soundly prepared. Again there was resistance from my 'steam' contemporaries, and again the Debating Society was one avenue for promoting new thinking over the widest possible spectrum. A newspaper extract from the *Yorkshire Evening Press* of 27 October 1958, tells the story:

YORK TO LONDON IN TWO & HALF HRS.

'QUITE PRACTICAL PROPOSITION'

The prospect of reducing the railway journey time from York to London to two-and-a-half hours is 'quite a practical proposition.'

Speaking to a meeting of the Federation of the North Eastern Regional Railway Lecture and Debating Societies, Mr F. L. Hick, assistant operating officer of the Region, said that the 22 Deltic-type diesel electric locomotives, some of which were already in service on major passenger routes, were reputed to be the most powerful locomotive British Railways had.

Although their introduction was an interim measure preceding electrification, the Deltics would be able to run at speeds comparable with electric locomotives.

MORE INTENSIVE

It was worth noting, Mr Hick continued, that the 22 Deltics were replacing 55 steam locomotives. This was an indication of the more intensive working and the economies being achieved by the change-over to diesel traction.

Mr Hick had earlier reviewed the progress made since the first diesel multiple units were introduced in 1955.

The public had responded quickly and permanently, he said, and the impact of the new mode of travel was unmistakeable.

Because it was new in every sense – 'a complete break from traditional railway practice' – it would help to bring business back to the railways.

FREIGHT SIDE

What was needed now was a stimulant on the freight side – 'something that captures the imagination, and is inherently good and business-like.'

Where diesels had been brought in, timing and punctuality had always improved considerably. Either-end drive, which made quick turn-rounds easier and reduced station movements and platform occupation, easy manipulation in emergencies, all helped towards improved operation.

For the railwaymen, fire, cleaning, coaling, watering – some of the dirtiest and most unpleasant railway work, were completely eliminated.

UNECONOMICAL LINES

Diesels, Mr Hick said, did provide a more economical form of working, but 'there should be no misunderstanding on anybody's part about diesel schemes which cannot properly pay their way.'

'They will have to be abandoned. With the modern trend of increased travel by private cars, motor cycles, etc, the use of railways in certain areas is likely to disappear.

'Therefore, there will undoubtedly be cases arising where even the more economical method of diesel rail operation will not save the branch lines from closure.'

This major transformation as described in my talk and referred to in the newspaper, from steam to diesel traction, and the implementation of new workings, new everything, was, as will be appreciated, of great significance to the railway scene as a whole and to the East Coast Regions in particular. It was a stupendous move towards the end of an era – a way of life was changing. And I was in the thick of it, helping to promote it – I believed in it and just got on with it. Coupled to that was the stepping up of branch line closures. The North Eastern lines were substantially still to the old pattern and intact, with local passenger services in plenty serving remote lines, goods trains ('pick-ups') still serving local stations, collieries in abundance still producing and using rail, busy docks, steelworks demanding large quotas of bolster wagons, and all round a demand for attention and direction. Staff had to be consulted on all these changes, and the public, through the Transport Users' Consultative Committees, had to be conferred with over branch line closures. It was all designed to help in the struggle for improved finances and to cope with the inevitable march of time.

If, during all this activity, you looked 'under the mat' you found a sense of foreboding. The worms at work. Road transport was taking advantage of inherent weaknesses in rail performance following the malaise of wartime neglect, which still persisted despite the infusion of some new equipment and new ideas. The 'costing' aspect, new in railway management, was drawing attention to individual unprofitable services resulting in shock withdrawal of many established workings and giving cause for comment by die-hards: 'What about their contribution to overheads, the removal of which undermined the profitability of other traffic?' So there were rumblings which warned of future discomfort, but some hope still there looking ahead to the days of electrification. It was a good job we didn't know it was still 30 years away.

But the foreboding also extended to personal relationships. It had become noticeable over the years how in railway circles heroes were created out of chiefs – the right kind of chiefs, of course – and this had happened in my experience. These heroes were not men who hit the high spots or went out to gather laurels. They were just sincere, dedicated chaps doing a job of work well and truly.

In 1960, my hero, chief and mentor, Lowingham Sproat, decided to retire. I was sad. Everybody was sad. But 'tempus fugit'. Who would succeed him in this key job? So many people asked me if I would like to. Of course I would, since it was the highest post in the Region in the 'Operating' world, a department in which I had spent most of my railway career, a phase of railway working I loved, was motivated by, and was very happy in. There were of course other contenders, especially from other Regions, while London HQ had some bright young competitors (I was 55 – now a retirement potential!). In addition, it was well known that I was not fully in support of the 'Divisional Management' form of organisation then being promoted, although I had made it clear that if it became management policy I would faithfully and emphatically honour it.

Why I did not favour it from the operating point of view was because I saw it destroying, or at least neutralising the direct line of responsibility from the chief operator to field level. It imposed another layer of communication, always a diluting element, between the person giving an instruction and the person who had the job of implementing it. Had I taken the pilot scheme appointment at Hull, my views might have been different, but here I was adjudicating from the operating angle, a situation calling for, as I have previously said, a 'doing' job, where I wanted loyalty and response undiluted. As it transpired, the national scheme of Divisional organisation was implemented in the North East with Divisional Managers at Newcastle, Middlesbrough, Leeds and Hull with their own Operating Assistants reporting to them who in turn reported to the General Manager with a 'tie' line to the Operating Officer at York headquarters. But as we all now know, this did not stand up to future needs. It took an experiment in Scotland in 1967/68 to show that the arrangement should be discontinued. It was concluded that this additional layer of organisation was expensive and unnecessary, and I could not help saying under my breath before I retired in 1969, 'I told you so'!

It was therefore a stormy passage to the job. I was interviewed three times and subjected to many questions as to my psychological approach to carrying out the function within the organisation laid down. I had given the matter a great deal of thought and pondered the proposed lines of communication time and time again, so I had to make it clear that I could not think one thing and say another. Loyalty to my management, however, was never in question, so I stuck to my guns and outlined my purpose should I be successful. Then one day Mr Short and Mr Margetts summoned me to the General Manager's office and seemed to take some delight in advising me that I had been appointed, despite everything(!), and all was well. I was very happy, not only because of a gratified ambition, but because of the marvellous family I was to inherit, all friends, many from my early days when I worked alongside them, people I knew gave their best in the interest of their job. I knew most of them in the office personally, over 250 of them, and I also knew many in the Districts with whom I had rubbed shoulders over the years. Never before had I been so thrilled with the genuine warmth of my reception to the new post, and those of us who have worked all our lives with railway staff know the extent to which this warmth and companionship gives a joy to living.

Soon I was to have Cliff Birch as my assistant – loyal, and a tower of strength – and the office organisation I took over was as shown in the accompanying diagram.

I believe there were about 40,000 staff in the Operating department of the Region when I took office, a massive figure made up from stations, marshalling yards, goods warehouses, docks, offices, colliery sidings, steel companies' sidings, and, of course, all the branch line operating staff which at that time (before Beeching) was substantial; it was by far the largest department, staff-wise, in the Region. With commitments of this size, we were bound to have staff problems over working conditions, rosters, individual grievances, and so on. Handling an extremely busy traffic situation, failings in performance due to shortcomings or human error were bound to arise. Though the smallest Region geographically, the North Eastern had the highest forwarded tonnage of freight of any other, and to hold the measures of performance at a good level, which we were doing, meant a tight rein on discipline and the maintenance of satisfactory staff relations.

The disputes which did arise through the union representatives were dealt with via the accepted channels, first in correspondence, and any which could be cleared by a sub-committee of the Sectional Council were so dealt with. Other items were referred to the main body of Sectional Council No 3 of which I was now Chairman.

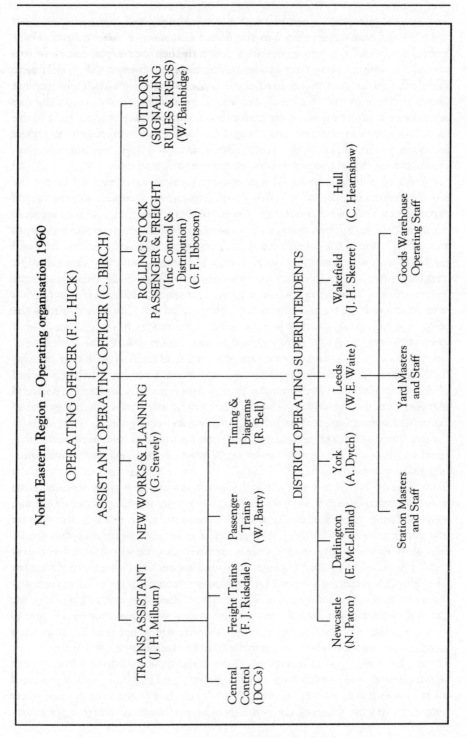

North Eastern Region – Operating organisation 1960

OPERATING OFFICER (F. L. HICK)

ASSISTANT OPERATING OFFICER (C. BIRCH)

TRAINS ASSISTANT
(J. H. Milburn)

NEW WORKS & PLANNING
(G. Stavely)

ROLLING STOCK
PASSENGER & FREIGHT
(Inc Control &
Distribution)
(C. F. Ibbotson)

OUTDOOR
(SIGNALLING
RULES & REGS)
(W. Bainbidge)

Central
Control
(DCCs)

Freight Trains
(F. J. Ridsdale)

Passenger
Trains
(W. Batty)

Timing &
Diagrams
(R. Bell)

DISTRICT OPERATING SUPERINTENDENTS

Newcastle
(N. Paton)

Darlington
(E. McLelland)

York
(A. Dytch)

Leeds
(W.E. Waite)

Wakefield
(J. H. Skerret)

Hull
(C. Hearnshaw)

Station Masters
and Staff

Yard Masters
and Staff

Goods Warehouse
Operating Staff

This council represented operating staff and was the regional negotiating platform of union and management for matters other than national staff interests, which were the responsibility of the Railways Board. When I first appeared before this committee, sitting opposite me as General Secretary of the staff side was Tommy Weighell, signalman at Northallerton and father of Sidney Weighell who became General Secretary of the NUR. He was a formidable figure, constructive, determined, a good negotiator. He understood and applied the true meaning of the word 'negotiate' – it did not mean 'negotiate' his views, full stop, any more than management should not mean 'negotiate' their views, full stop – but truly negotiate on and through the subject as a whole, an important distinction.

I also took the chair when the staff of other councils were involved along with No 3, as, for example, when closure of branch lines, which affected most departments' staff, were concerned. These were large meetings, sometimes with emotional overtones, with individuals wanting to make their name, and sometimes succeeding! I found this stimulating, and during my term of office found the 'staff' representatives were most responsive, though at times of course very determined to gain their point. It was in these circumstances that I followed Sir Mark Hodgson's advice and his 'tips' on negotiation, which were invaluable. I had a very good relationship with the men, no doubt helped by the fact that I had worked with some of them at 'ground' level, that I was an old 'North Eastern Railway' man, as were some of the staff side, and was interested in them as individuals, and this concern lasted with some long after my retirement. In fact, as the only senior officer who had joined the old North Eastern Railway, I was asked in the 1960s to be Chairman of the NE Railway Servants Pension Society (previously chaired by the General Manager), on the committee of which were former wages grade staff members of Sectional Council. I am still, in 1991, a trustee of the society and make no secret of the fact that it is a matter of great joy that I continue to meet my former signalman, guard and driver friends regularly and, I hope, make a contribution to the well-being of pensioner colleagues.

In September 1951 my family and I were on holiday at a small Spanish resort called LLaFranc (Costa Brava), at a tiny hotel with no other English people in the area. (It had not yet been discovered!) One day we climbed a hill to a lighthouse and from a corner of a room I heard an English voice. A delightful English couple who were holidaying in the next village immediately made our acquaintance, and took us in their car up that gorgeous coast to Tamariu and Ague Blava. One may ask, 'Why this comment in an otherwise railway orientated book?' Because this was the meeting of John Gratwick, a senior member of the consultancy firm of Urwick Orr and Partners, and myself. I omit the intervening years when our friendship was personal, when our friendship grew, when 'consulting' was not used by railways, to move on to the time when my appreciation of consultants' work became better known, and I asked John, 'What could "consultancy" do for railways?' We thought of management, use of manpower and equipment at stations and goods depots, and all the potential of railway working. We already had 'razor gangs', work-study people, and trouble-shooters, but here I thought was inquiry on a higher plane, and

I turned to Freddie Margetts, Assistant General Manager (Traffic) and my boss.

As a result we arranged to meet John Gratwick officially in Leeds where he had his office and staff. From then on, FCM followed up the matter with the General Manager and no doubt others concerned, with the result that Urwick Orr and Partners were commissioned to report on not only the matters I had put forward but also on other activities relating to the Region and the railways as a whole. Readers will no doubt have heard of instances where consultants have been introduced by an executive to find in due course that he himself is displaced. It took a year or two for this to happen to me, as I will explain later. Meanwhile, that chance meeting at a Spanish lighthouse resulted in highly critical reports following highly critical investigations, shaking NE top management and permeating through to BTC headquarters. Such is life!

As an operating chief for the Region I automatically became a member of the BTC Operating Committee under the chairmanship of John Vipond. He was followed by Gerry Fiennes and later by Lance Ibbotson during my membership. We met once a month in London and it was a useful channel of communication both official and unofficial, since a lot of discussion took place amongst members outside the conference room. We compared notes on interpretation of policies and sometimes found solutions to everyday problems, especially freight movement problems, that could not be achieved in correspondence or over the phone. Occasionally we had cause to visit and report on a special project; for example, we went to the Dowty establishment to witness their new idea for braking freight wagons in marshalling yards; this was a proposal for Tinsley new yard where sidings were to be fitted with hydraulic plungers with automatically retarded wagons as they proceeded along the siding, thus reducing or eliminating impact with other wagons. The committee was also a medium for keeping us informed of BTC thinking, or rather of the Chief Operating Officer's thinking, on matters concerning our department.

A daily work feature was the 'morning report' when all Regional Operating Officers came together on the telephone with the Chief Operating Officer at HQ and exchanged information on the 'state of the nation'. Accidents, if any, were reported upon, together with serious delays to passenger trains or freight movements, problems with wagon supplies and, believe it or not, a favourite nuisance, shortage of freight guards' vans which could seriously affect mobility of freight traffic. Action to put matters right was agreed, such action being mandatory, and the results were reviewed the following day. Preparing for this review meant a visit to Central Control at 8.30 am, where the Trains Assistant and Deputy Chief Controller had gathered the required information and indicated forward prospects and what was being done. Obviously much of the field of discussion centred on inter-regional working, hence the need for inter-regional analysis. I understand that the conference still goes on daily, having survived many changes in operating practices!

An interesting inquiry in July 1961, in which I participated along with Fred Margetts and Bill Golding, Transport Manager of Dorman Long Steel (Tees-side), was concerned with the proposed conveyance by rail of molten metal between Tees-side and Consett Iron Works. We visited Dusseldorf (Krupps), Western Germany, where a scheme was in operation whereby molten metal was poured from the furnace into specially constructed wagons, and conveyed some distance over main lines under closely regulated movement instructions. The steel works chief was most helpful; we were shown the complete process, and supplied with all the information we required. We also examined steel transport arrangements, the type of wagons used, and loading facilities and stacking methods of steel in various forms preparatory to loading on to rail wagons. It was a highly efficient process and we were impressed by many features, especially the handling methods in the storage yards, and the rail wagon loading facilities.

We afterwards visited steel works in Luxemburg and Longwy (France), gathering useful information, much of which we were able to make use of in the North East. Bill Golding, a former traffic apprentice on the NER, was a most constructive and co-operative business colleague, as well as being a personal friend. Traffic to and from his and other Tees-side steel firms was enormous, and it was in all our interests to maintain a constant liaison with them. The twice-yearly meeting with the senior people representing the North East steelmakers at the Zetland Hotel, Saltburn, was always a memorable occasion.

One evening in 1961, travelling by cab from King's Cross to a meeting of the Institute of Transport, Mr Short, Mr Margetts (no first names for seniors in those days!) and myself were discussing the uncomfortable volume of complaints which were being levelled at the railways, and we came to the conclusion that we in the North East should go out and meet the public. I was thereupon nominated to present the case for the railways with F.C.M. in the chair. The launching pad was to be Huddersfield, where much criticism of the West Riding services, both local and main line, and also freight, was being conducted through the press and other channels. A large hall was hired, the meeting date advertised, and we waited.

In the event the hall was packed, and I presented our case and our purpose in meeting the public. The case was based on the continuing drain of wartime needs of which the general public had no conception, but was brightened by the hopes of the Modernisation Plan, some details of which were given. The discussion was, as expected, very lively, some supporting our aims and understanding much of our problem, while some vigorously attacked us, one so much that I threw out a challenge to him that I would meet him in debate anywhere, any time on a public platform on this very subject. Needless to say I am still waiting! But the audience – our customers – liked the idea!.

The evident success of that meeting led to the holding of similar meetings (though without a formal address, merely an introduction by the Chairman and a 'question time') throughout the Region, where large attendances proved the value of 'meeting the public'. A panel of speakers was arranged in each District, District Officers being included as necessary. A touch of humour helped on occasions, as when at Harrogate a speaker said of a delay on a cold rainy evening, 'There we were waiting on the station platform until puddles began to appear down the line of the crowd'. I couldn't resist saying, 'No wonder puddles appeared after so long – you were but human!' Dr Beeching approved of these meetings and Freddie said that they were helpful in getting him appointed to the Board!

One of the duties of the head of the Operating department is organising and accompanying royal journeys, and I described some of the arrangements in an earlier chapter. The railway liaison with the Royal Household was in London and essential information about a proposed royal journey over North Eastern Region lines were conveyed to my office, when I was consulted as to detailed timings, choice of overnight stop (if required) and liaison with civic authorities; a draft programme was then prepared and submitted for Palace approval. When approval was received, the appropriate routine was applied and all concerned brought into the picture. If the journey was made over NE lines, it was my duty to travel with the train as officer in charge. Obviously I had to satisfy myself that the trainmen had all the information and instructions for the journey, that the train control staff were fully aware of the need to keep the path clear, and that signalmen and other staff concerned were alerted. I travelled on trains conveying most members of the Royal Family during my period of office, and became acquainted with many of the royal staff concerned with their travel needs. Where civic visits were involved, along with railway requirements I had to meet the Town Clerk or other equivalent civic official prior to such visits to ensure a close liaison between railway and local authority. If it entailed a visit to a railway establishment it was necessary to fix details of the route, presentation of people and all the incidentals which make a royal visit successful.

Most journeys passed without undue incident, though on one occasion, when Her Majesty was travelling up from Scotland to London, the train was stopped by signals north of Morpeth. I quickly got to a telephone to learn that there was a suspected broken rail in the section ahead. Delay to a Royal Train was unwelcome to say the least, but safety had to come first and something had to be done quickly. A down train, travelling in the opposite direction, was therefore stopped, and the local Station Master and a permanent way man were put on the engine to scrutinise the up line, the driver proceeding slowly. A detached fishplate was discovered and rectified, the down train then proceeded and I was informed. I instructed the driver of the Royal Train to exercise special caution up to the next signal box. Visions of single line working and all that that entailed had loomed up in my mind while waiting for the down train – but I was saved!

I had a number of journeys with the 'Queen Mum' and it was a great pleasure to witness her stoicism when, her train having been stabled overnight at Ponteland (north of Newcastle), she had sprained her ankle, but had to launch a ship at Wallsend. Nothing daunted, she did her duty from an invalid chair handled from and to the train by her staff, with great acclamation from the crowd nearby.

But the most outstanding assignment in this context was in connection with the wedding of the Duke and Duchess of Kent in 1961. My department, through the District Officer and the York Station Master, Harry Thompson, was responsible for the railway arrangements at York and Malton stations and over the North Eastern running lines. My contacts with the civic chiefs beforehand (Tom Benfield was York's Town Clerk and was always helpful as well as being a great guy) settled the location of representatives meeting the royal party, the red carpet, the seating of privileged spectators and the decoration of the station and its precincts.

History was being created in that this was the conveyance by train of the largest number of royalty in one movement – two full trains of crowned heads and their families, and another train-load of royal guests all converging on York station in as close succession as possible. So all eyes were on the action. To cheer me up somebody reminded me of the time when King Edward VII was arriving at York station by train and the signalman responsible at Locomotive Box turned the Royal Train into the wrong platform away at the far side of the station, instead of into the platform near the station hotel entrance (being used on this occasion) and where the red carpet was placed. Imagine the consternation and chagrin of railway officers and others waiting to receive His Majesty who had to hurry over the bridge to meet him and explain the mistake! I heard the story often from Sid Moody, whose father was the signalman concerned.

The Royal Station Hotel lounge was the waiting place and communications centre, where representatives of all parties concerned, including the royal household, gathered. I had my own information channel through the train control system who kept me advised of the progress of the trains, cheerfully running on time. Forty-five minutes before the first train was due I received an SOS from the royal representatives saying that Lord Snowdon had lost his white carnation button hole, and would we get a replacement by the time the train arrived at York? I looked around for the young man at my disposal, Ron Duke, and asked him to go on his motorbike to Challis Nurseries for half a dozen white carnations.

He was back in no time with the carnations, gathered in a small basket, and handed them to me. I was on the platform waiting the arrival of the first train, in which Lord Snowdon was travelling, when I was called away and hurriedly put the basket down beside one of the huge pillars as a landmark as to its whereabouts when I returned. But on returning the basket had gone – vanished. Aghast, and looking around for inspiration, I saw amongst the railway officers and their wives six superb carnations adorning their dresses and suits. Sydney Jesper, our PR & PO admitted seeing them and, not realising what they were for, had shared them out amongst his pals! He had no idea I possessed the scale of language I delivered to him privately – he never lived it down. The arrangements made for getting the blooms to Lord Snowdon worked, and when he stepped from the train wearing his buttonhole I knew all was well!

Most importantly, the whole of the York plan worked without falter and we all rejoiced in the wedding of our Yorkshire bride to the royal Duke in the superb setting of York Minster.

The next phase of the operation was to see the empty trains to Malton where, following the reception at Hovingham Hall, the royal travellers were to join their trains for London. Again, arrangements had to be 'spot on', with the passengers, all of them, monitored through the narrow entrance, on to the confined space of a narrow platform and into the appropriate train. Somehow it worked! I travelled on the first train from Malton in a compartment near the Royal family, and Prince Charles (then a boy of about 12 years) came along to ask a number of questions, mostly about the railway and the arrangements for the day. I was very pleased he took so much interest in what was taking place.

Five minutes out of Malton, the catering staff panicked because, rather belatedly, they had discovered that there was no whisky in the restaurant car, so I threw a note out at the first signal box we came to and the signalman passed the message to York. The day was saved! Two bottles were to hand on arrival at York where Gerry Fiennes was waiting to take over the train to King's Cross. Gerry was then Line Manager, King's Cross Eastern Region (Great Northern).

The drivers and guards who controlled the actual movements of the trains were great in performance, and proud, as we all were, to be concerned with such an outstanding event.

Another important contact of national implication was with the military and other defence organisations. Movement of Army, Navy and Air Force personnel had a special channel of approach which had been used before and after the war. There was an understanding between the railways and War Office that so far as the North of England was concerned the operating chief would be the official liaison with the GOC, Northern Command, York. This I knew had applied over a very long period, for when as a young man I had been in the Programme office, special 'Secret' files were held there in locked drawers, documenting the proposed 'troop' train schedules in time of mobilisation. A member of the staff had the job of timing and agreeing the train plan with the transport officer of the Northern Command. That arrangement still held when I became Operating Officer, and I met the responsible Colonel annually to review the situation.

Each Monday during 1961 there were lunchtime talks in the Board Room to which I contributed. They were well supported by staff and were frequently used to describe the functions of various departments, to comment on progress (or otherwise) of projects in hand, or to launch ideas, thus spreading information across the railway population. It was also an avenue for expressing criticism if anyone wished to do so, thus giving an opportunity to counter, explain or amplify on a subject.

I encouraged the social side of the office too, and regretted that soon after my term as head of the department ended, the hierarchy seemed to lose interest in that aspect of human relations. I agree that circumstances were changing – there were substantial staff reductions and the railways generally were losing ground.

I recall that both before the war and after we had in York an annual 'Railway Ball'. Sponsored from the General Manager's office, it was held in the Assembly Rooms, that gorgeous Georgian setting, when top railway people and civic dignitaries and guests gave status and lustre to our existence. All staff were welcome and it was always a 'full house', with London officers travelling down for the event and helping to make it an occasion. To many it was the social event of the year.

Office outings in all departments were approved, and sometimes special trains were provided at a small cost to the staff, but the main advantage was that on those days a 'mixing' process took place and the seniors got to know the juniors and vice versa. The outings involved the majority of the staff from a department (a skeleton staff was left in the office) and they went in a party to the Dales, Lake District, Moors, etc, for a day in spring or summer. The organisers of these trips competed from year to year to produce a 'better than last year' event. It generated a marked 'esprit de corps', a vital element in the output of one's organisation.

But later these outings, together with the annual office socials (usually dinner, dance and games), ceased. A cold, steely atmosphere permeated from the top, and cornerstones were steadily removed from the community fabric of the establishment. The infinitesimal price of such things was being rated more highly than their morale promotion value. The change in attitudes consequently reduced morale. I realised that staff conditions had changed, that Saturday morning working had gone and some compensations were in place, but if life is to be worth living a 'close' feeling needs to be generated within any group of working human beings. And by that I do not mean a slackening of discipline.

Another forced lapse, this time during my period of office, was the Best Kept Station Competition, a movement which motivated station staff to keep premises generally clean and orderly, and particularly to make, improve, and beautify the station garden. The result with some stations was spectacular. If there was someone, it might be the Station Master, his wife, or one of the staff, who was knowledgeable and enthusiastic about gardening, the dullest station could, at negligible cost, be transformed, and passengers and the local press would applaud. Each year in summer there was an inspection. It was for me to appoint two judges who were required in a three weeks' tour to examine each station which had entered for the competition, and inspect the buildings. They were to pay special attention to toilets, waiting rooms and so on, but most of all to judge the garden for colour, variety of plants, and the overall picture, taking into account also the environmental and topographical difficulties which may have been encountered.

Two stalwarts were invited to judge during the last three years of the competition, Tom Wooding, formerly Revenue Accountant from the railway offices in Newcastle, who lived in Stocksfield, and Dick Garth, Assistant Civil Engineer, York. They were both retired, knew the ropes, and were knowledgeable on gardening. Concerning weeds, Dick Garth was often 'chivvied' about his being Engineer for the Derwent Valley Light Railway (freight only), where the line was smothered in weeds. Why did they not keep the route clear? 'Because weeds hold the line together!' What better justification than that? The judges did not receive any fee but, of course, if they stayed overnight they received out-of-pocket expenses. They travelled the Region in my inspection saloon carriage (No 902179) hauled by an appropriate engine. They worked to a predetermined plan, sometimes the loco propelling the saloon, the timings of the 'garden special' being issued in a separate working notice. The train was described as an 'Officer's Special', and I remember when I was in the Programme office every working notice contained an 'Officer's special' trip, they were then so frequently used. It was the only means of officers visiting sites or outstations in those days, and saloons were allocated to some Districts as well as headquarters officers.

The area covered by the 'garden special' stretched from Berwick in the north to Shaftholme Junction in the south, and considerable interest was shown in the results which were published in the monthly NE Magazine. District Officers and other officials were invited to accompany the special over territory in which they were interested, and the General Manager would make at least one visit (when I accompanied him) to demonstrate his interest in the scheme. Mr Kitson, sometime a Director of the old North Eastern Railway and later on the NE Area Board, liked to go up to the Hawes branch and see the wonderful displays in the gardens up there. The competition had the effect of keeping stations in good trim and there was also publicity value, especially locally – alas to no avail in keeping such stations open. Accompanying each journey was my head office messenger, who acted as guard, a post for which he was qualified. He was responsible for stocking the saloon with victuals obtained from either railway hotels or refreshment rooms, and looking after the needs of guests on board. I understand that that particular saloon is still in existence at Carnforth.

With the closing of branch lines going on apace amidst the economic blizzard then prevailing, I saw the end of these inspections, and travelled on the last journey, which was over East Riding territory. We were timed to return from Bridlington to York over the Driffield-Market Weighton line, shortly to be closed, and I asked the driver if he would, as he passed through Bainton station, give three 'crows' on the whistle of his locomotive, in deference to my service there and as a mark of respect to its demise. Sic (or Hic) transit gloria mundi . . .

Safety on the line and reliability in performance were always my first priority. Having been a Signalman's Inspector, I knew the pitfalls which were so often just around the corner. I therefore arranged with the District Officers a series of personal visits to each District to talk on the subject directly to Inspectors who were required to take charge of the working after an accident or, particularly, had to supervise the introduction of special working for permanent way work, renewal of bridges, or signalling alterations and renewals, and to check upon completion that all was in proper working order. My emphasis was on the precautions necessary and the need for special care under these conditions. It was a new departure in the NE for the headquarters operating chief thus to talk directly with District Inspectors, but in addition to getting a message across it also enabled me to assess the quality of our safety specialists, the men on the ground.

It had been in my mind for some time after I returned to the Operating department that we were short of people, at both District and headquarters, who had a specialist knowledge of signalling and Rules and Regulations; men who could interpret the full significance of that extremely important aspect of train working, who were capable of critically analysing what was going on around them when out on the line or during an emergency, or running a station or a marshalling yard, and who were qualified to draw up working instructions to appear in a detailed notice relating to abnormal conditions. I thought we should have a short and intensive educational programme for a selected few who had ambition and had showed interest in the subject, and thereby hold a torch, as it were, to greater concern for the subject.

After receiving the blessing of staff colleagues, six young men from various grades were appointed. Amongst those selected was a fireman and a signalman, while the rest were clerical staff, and they were designated 'signalling trainees'. We designed a curriculum based on traffic apprentice lines, where the candidates moved around and gained an insight into the various aspects of the subject, including a period with Inspectors. Arthur Wigram, Signals Engineer, gladly welcomed the suggestion that the trainees should spend some time in his department in turn, and this proved a valuable experience. It gave them an insight into the technical features of signalling, a useful adjunct to the operating knowledge, and something that most of us had been required to pick up as we went along.

The candidates had to report currently on their activities to a section chief, and were interviewed by me every few weeks so that I could keep in touch with their progress. At the end of their training I was satisfied that the experiment had been worthwhile, and that we were fortified with some people who were really proficient in their knowledge of the safety requirements and techniques of operating practices. They stimulated thought on the subject as they moved around and, from their comments to me, they helped to convey a feeling of professionalism in the grades concerned. They were also sought-after for appointments, and one or two of them may still be in the service.

Of prime concern to the job was the contact and relationship with the Ministry of Transport Inspectorate. New works involving the safety of the line, such as new signal boxes and new signalling schemes, including new systems (eg level crossing barriers), had to receive the blessing of the MOT people and discussions with them were arranged accordingly. It was on these occasions that I sometimes used the inspection saloon allocated to me, which was always 'at the ready' in a special 'saloon' shed, cleaned and maintained. For new signalling schemes this method of inspection was particularly suitable.

Reportable accidents also had to receive my personal attention, and of course it was my duty to attend and contribute to Ministry inquiries. There were occasions when I was asked to attend at the Ministry of Transport offices in London to give a full account of an accident and so avoid a full-scale inquiry which would have had to be dealt with otherwise. This could only apply when the mishap was a minor one.

When I was head of Passenger Train section I was, as previously mentioned, concerned with carriage design. Now I was in charge of an important section dealing with both carriage and wagon design, and building programmes which were pursued in conjunction with the BRB. We were required to prepare the NER case, with, in certain respects, the Eastern Region in an annual review on the coaching stock side – items such as open stock versus compartmented stock, furnishing, types of coupling (screw or buck-eye), braking systems (vacuum or air), seating, ventilation, cleaning, spare stock for special trains, Pullman requirements, nameboards, and a multitude of other items.

Similarly on the freight side, with private ownership of wagons for specific traffic beginning to appear, special considerations arose. Private coal wagons were commonplace and tight control of all types was the aim of the central wagon control introduced some few years earlier by C. M. Jenkin Jones. I had lived with the intricacies of ensuring the control which was necessary when in the District and in the Controls. No greater sin could be committed by a Station Master or other person responsible for compiling the daily wagon report than to misrepresent his wagon position to solve an availability difficulty. Many sleuths were employed by this section at times of severe wagon shortage to check up on these reports, and many supervisors of all ranks have 'exploded' at the discovery of hidden treasure! In any case, I had to keep in touch with such matters in relation to the traffic position as a whole.

11.

OFF WITH THE OLD AND ON WITH THE NEW

The consultants, Urwick, Orr and Partners, whom I introduced to our organisation, expanded their inquiries, at the request of management, to a wider field than originally intended, into the traffic departments, especially 'operating' or, as they preferred to call it 'movements'. I devoted many hours and days helping, explaining the work from top to bottom, and surrendered one of my very able assistants, Ewart Waite, to help them full time. To what extent the consultants' views were considered by the Railway Executive on a national basis in their commitment to a policy of decentralisation I do not know, but it soon became apparent to me that my function was to be diluted, my department split into two parts – operation and planning – working sideways to Divisional Managers, and upwards to a new appointment, Assistant General Manager (Movements). This new concept was leading to a position which I had suspected was in the making. They, the Board management, were moving the goal-posts. I stood to be displaced, as eventually I was, to be appointed Movements Planning Manager.

The new post of AGM (Movements) was up for grabs, but I was not acceptable because of my age (they call it ageism now!), so I was 'confidentially' told later, coupled with the fact that I had not been a District Officer. And, it was added, any appointment was designed to be a stepping stone to higher things – hence a younger man. I must admit that as my opposite numbers in other Regions were appointed, I was disappointed, to put it mildly. Taking a large, juicy mouthful of sour grapes, may I say that it took three short-lived successive appointments to fulfil that General Manager's prognostications about the post being a stepping stone to higher places. I make no comment on the so-called management 'appointment' skills presumably brought into play on each of those occasions.

Really I should have expected this since the General Manager at the time, a former civil engineer, and I had problems. Our chemistry did not mix – at all. He had, at times, instructed me to do certain things in the operating field which I had found difficult to accept. For example, on an occasion of timetable revision he knew that a meeting of the East Coast Passenger Train Committee (in which the Eastern, North Eastern and Scottish Regions were involved) was due, and told me to include in the NE proposals a plan to give greater frequency of service to and from London by running a number of trains composed of portions from Newcastle, Leeds and Hull, to be joined up to form one train south from Doncaster, the work of combining or splitting, depending on the direction, to be done in Doncaster station, then purely Eastern Region. He requested to see the plan my staff had prepared under my direction, and approving it asked me to press it forward at the meeting, despite my protestations.

Anyone who knows anything about passenger train working would throw up their hands in horror at the thought of a three-portion working on a main trunk route. It would be suicidal! So off I went to the meeting thinking about my own credibility among the experts! Geoff Coaker was in the chair, and I presented the scheme as instructed for consideration and development. Doncaster was his responsibility and, as expected, and with his innate courtesy, he firmly turned it down. He could not countenance such an arrangement and the subsequent minutes which his own General Manager had to endorse dealt with the matter appropriately.

I regret to say that there were occasions when the GM and I were in open conflict, something I had never before experienced in my career. Two of these cases related to senior staff in my department being seriously called into question as to their performance based, as it transpired, on either wrong information or wrong assumption. I found this very disturbing.

On the reorganisation question, I could never understand the logic of taking the timing and diagramming from the jurisdiction of the chief operator, since it was so easy at an inquest on punctuality for the timetable planner to say: 'The operator accepted my plan when submitted – over to him'. Anyhow, I understand that it is now back in its rightful place. The planner has to justify his own plan in performance.

I now concentrated on planning, and foremost on the stocks was a huge development programme by the Central Electricity Generating Board necessitating rail facilities. Starting with the building of a power station at Leeds, there were to follow in sequence Ferrybridge (major extension), Eggborough (new) and Drax (new), all on the Aire & Calder Canal and in the North Eastern Region. The sites were selected because of their proximity to coal supplies, rail facilities and water. They were all to be planned for 'merry-go-round' working by rail between colliery and power station, a shuttle system of working first introduced in the North East for conveyance of imported iron ore between Tyne Dock and Consett iron works. The CEGB consulted us right from the birth of the idea as to where their new stations should be located, and I was involved with their senior planning people building up the case for each project in our Region. We drew up in detail terminal layouts to suit the topography at each plant and the mechanical discharge of wagons in full train loads, and planned all the railway around this CEGB need for an 'endless belt' system of transport. The latest techniques in signalling and discharging equipment were tried and tested, and it has to be said that the type of wagon with is appurtenances which had to be specially designed and produced was one of the most difficult aspects to resolve. In fact, an engineering expert on wagon design (Maddison) concentrated on getting the best type possible from all angles – carrying capacity, braking system, bottom door discharge, interior lining to facilitate quick and smooth discharge in all weather conditions with differing kinds of coal, couplings, and robustness to withstand the intense use of the fleet.

With the development of the policy of full-train-load working came the idea of petrol in bulk from and to specially built and equipped terminals. Leading this development was Terry House who came from Shell and with whom I had some contact concerning the terminal facilities at Leeds and the approach lines from Neville Hill. It was an exciting innovation which eventually grew into a long-term business and pointed the way for other traffics. I have to say unfortunately that House may have been (and was) a good marketeer, but he was an unpopular man in the Regions where he treated quite senior officers with 'bounce'.

But to return to the 'merry-go-round' trains, we had to consider the type of loading facilities at collieries which were required to match the new wagon and train operation at the actual dispatch point, needing the same careful planning co-operation between the various parties. Also, synchronising with the introduction of each scheme there had to be adjustments to the location of train crews, causing transfer of rosters from one depot to another, matters which at the time caused some heartache. However, once the teething troubles were overcome, and once the trainmen and colliery terminal staff had mastered the continuous movement of the trains during actual discharge, there was a sense of achievement. As with the introduction of the first DMUs, to see in due course these 'merry-go-round' trains working at collieries and power stations was stimulating. It was a new dimension in the co-operation of three major industries, coal, electricity and railways, in the performance field, one which has survived over the years and has contributed to the finances of all three.

Meanwhile, great things were happening. Lord Beeching had come and gone. Sir Stanley Raymond was now Chairman of the Board and told us about the proposed combination of the Eastern and North Eastern Regions. He called the senior officers of both Regions to a lunch at Liverpool Street, thumped on the table and assured us all that none of us would suffer in consequence. He would give his personal assurance on that. Within a short time he was sacked by Barbara Castle, Minister of Transport, and Bill (later Sir Henry) Johnson succeeded him, a popular choice (he hadn't been a District Officer either!). Branch lines were being closed following the 'Reshaping' policy of the great Doctor, which within five or so years resulted in the withdrawal of one-third of the route mileage run by passenger trains, and closed about 1,700 passenger stations throughout the system – a big slice of responsibility gone. Marshalling yards were being severely pruned and freight train operations curtailed in many directions to reflect the deteriorating traffic flow. Considerable economies were called for and were achieved by staff under my jurisdiction who had the detailed job, in conjunction with Divisional Managers, of investigating the possibilities and drawing up the plans. These plans I had to present to meetings of the officers concerned and, subject to any alteration, put into the processing pot. It was a busy but, to me, highly negative process, but nevertheless inevitable.

But there were some positive things I had to do when the Eastern and North Eastern merged and I became 'Special Projects Officer' (which really meant 'spare'!), and they were (1) freightliner development and the (2) provision and development of a 'container base' at Leeds. I was to assist the freightliner organisation when T. G. Gibb, a former North Eastern man, was in charge, working with such able people as Tim Bolland, Gerry Burt and David Cobbet. I contributed to the development of the depots at Tyneside, Stockton, Leeds, Hull, Felixstowe and Tilbury – the location of the sites, the facilities to be provided, layout and train workings were all involved. My greatest dissension within the programme was in respect of the location of the Hull depot. I contended that it should be on the docks but found, despite the presentation of considerable evidence to that end, that the port authorities would not support the idea. In fact, I contended that Hull, with its extensive waterfront, docks and large standing areas, with drive and entrepreneurial approach, had enormous potential to rival Felixstowe which was then struggling in its early stages. However, the port manager was quite adamant, and the depot was built elsewhere in Hull in accordance with policy, but did not thrive.

The idea of freightliner operations appealed. The economics which motivated its adoption as a profitable undertaking were not available to me, but I was to help in its development, especially from the planning side, by contributing to layout and other facilities to be provided for a series of depots. I was also required to assist in the opening up process of a new depot. When I came on the scene, therefore, policy had been decided, and the location of the first depots, based on an analysis of traffic flows, agreed, with the further prospect of additional sites to be built up as the scheme unfolded. Being non-technical, I did not become involved in the provision of the mechanical appliances needed to lift the containers.

The early days were fraught with physical problems. The lifting gear, despite the engineers' efforts to secure the best available, frequently failed. Suitable containers were in short supply, and in fact there was a problem in the design of the carrying vehicles which reacted on terminal working where efforts were made to make up the shortcomings. Costs rose in terms of both staff and equipment, while estimates of potential traffic had been too optimistic. Meanwhile, the commercial people were talking in terms of attracting more road hauliers to use the service, but the unions objected and even took strike action. They thought that encouraging hauliers to use rail would somehow react on their staffing levels – the men on the ground at some of the depots couldn't agree, so there was a muddle, not a good omen for the future. It was depressing to see this happening to what many of us thought was a new dimension in freight transport, and which had given hope of a renaissance in the movement by rail of the higher classes of goods. The special trains travelling at speed were hailed as only the start, but the union intervention, the higher costs and the innate problems in operation all eventually persuaded the BRB, along with the government, to transfer the whole outfit to the National Freight Corporation.

In hindsight, the unions must surely regret their obstructive action. Given a longer term for development, concentrated research and loyalty from the staff, there must be a future somewhere in this direction. It would appear there must soon come an equivalent, to relive trunk roads of the current chronic congestion if wholesale seizures in those arteries are to be avoided.

My final planning job was monitoring the rail aspect, in conjunction with OCL and Associated Containers Ltd, of the building of their Leeds container base. It was their initiative and we planned from scratch an establishment to cater for rail, road and sea traffic in international containers; it was one of a number of depots these firms were building throughout the country. The land on which the building was to stand was part of the site we on the railway had originally earmarked for a new marshalling yard at Stourton, and was adjacent to the freightliner depot which it was intended to use substantially for overseas traffic going through British ports. I understand that the depot, now called an Inland Customs Clearance Depot, is successful, and with the advent of the Channel Tunnel the advanced thinking of those whose idea it was in the first place has been fully justified.

It is hoped that the reader does not interpret my story as being an egotist's idea of splendid isolation. Egotistic – yes. Splendid isolation – no! Railway operation can only be successful if it is shared amongst a number of people with one objective – to achieve. Nowhere else in railway performance does so much depend on the co-operation of our fellow men. Consequently much time and effort must necessarily be spent consulting partners in the service. Staff like to be consulted as to what is expected of them, and other officers too. The Commercial Officer, to be as certain as you can that you are providing what he wants; the Civil Engineer, that he is providing the track that you want; the Signal Engineer, that he too is giving the facilities in signalling techniques to meet your operating requirements; the Mechanical Engineer, who provides the power to enable you to do anything at all. So it will be evident that the Operating chief and his staff must at all times be available and amenable to open discussion. That was my objective throughout and constituted an important part of my philosophy.

12.

STONESTAR, AND RETIREMENT

It must have been noticeable to the reader that since I lost my operating job, my story has lost some of its verve. This is inevitable. From then on my work, always a joy, became less positive. But that was only from a business angle. When I saw the trend of things, I decided to prepare for my retirement. Most officers up to now had said 'out' at 65, but I put a limit of 64 – and 64 it was. Meanwhile, however, I developed a new love.

The Lake District had always been my main leisure attraction when I could get away – my wife came from Windermere – and I knew the area very well. I had climbed the mountains and walked the fells, experienced their moods, fished the streams. I now wanted a hidy-hole so that I could revel in a new environment and start what was to be a new life. So we, the family, went looking, looking. One day we found a 'place with a view' – ideal – and to all intents and purposes empty and deserted. My elder son found a way in and with a 'whoops' opened the front door. We had been told by a local farmer, who also said that it was empty, that it belonged to an old lady who had been taken to a home 12 years earlier, and she had not been back since. We went in.

The hall was empty except for a superb grandfather clock, tucked away in the corner. The kitchen had utensils round the sink with kitchen furniture in position. The sitting room was empty. But the dining room! On the table was a solid silver salver worth a mint! Other dining silver and valuable crockery was in the cupboards. Drink in uncorked bottles. Antique furniture with patches of mould placed round a priceless table. And there, thrown casually over a chair back, was the lady's raincoat, as if on departure it had been left by mistake. Upstairs in what must have been the lady's bedroom, the bed had been turned back, no doubt left just as she had got out of it 12 years previously. The moths had had a field day, and the whole of the bedclothes were decomposing in a ruinous heap. It was weird, uncanny, and sent a shiver down my back! We felt guilty at the intrusion, but compelled to complete the survey.

We hurriedly inquired of the farmer about the lady owner. He was amazed to hear of our experience and told us that the local solicitor at Broughton-in-Furness was the most likely man to inform us, so off we went posthaste to report and apologise. We found him in a small room surrounded by a mass of paper – he could hardly find his telephone when it rang. He certainly couldn't find the relevant papers for the house, but after much fishing around I found them in a wilderness of files! He listened to the story without getting too excited, but agreed that something should be done. How the place had escaped burglary or vandalism was a tribute to the local population. We told him that we would like to purchase the property if and when it came up for sale. To cut a long story short, the house was quickly cleared and, as the old lady was not to return, it was sold to the highest bidder – which was not me! It was advertised nationally and the London people made the running – so that was that.

However, my farmer friend told me of another old place which had not been lived in for 36 years. Sheep had made the downstairs rooms their shelter. Rats abounded. There were hundreds of bats in the roof, which was falling in. Almost derelict, it had been built in 1700, with a built-in date plaque to confirm the fact. But what a position!

Overlooking the Duddon Valley, it stood off the Ulpha road, hidden behind rocks, with only a rough track as access, no water supply except a spring in a wood nearby, and no electricity of course. There was no other habitation in sight except a white farmhouse far away on the other side of the valley; Black Coombe, perhaps the oldest mountain in the country, rose away to the left, the Duddon river down below. Its name – 'Stonestar' – appeared on the Ordnance Survey map, and it was described in the survey I had done by a professional surveyor as a yeoman farmer's former house. This surveyor closed his report by saying that it was only fit for demolition and rebuilding.

We saw the potential, but the landlord who owned the estate covering the lower part of the valley would not then sell. But after a year's efforts working on his agent who lived at Ravenglass, we came to an arrangement and eventually a sale. Ignoring pessimists and optimists alike, we set to work on restoring the old place. Our sons, their friends, our friends, local well-wishers, wives, their friends – anybody with a pair of hands was enlisted, and what a wonderful place emerged! When it was habitable, most of my colleagues from York and their wives came to christen it and we had nearly 20 years of great enjoyment from it. It replaced my interest and concentration on what had been a life's work on the railway, and directed my enthusiasm elsewhere. But as with my railway, my wife and I had to surrender even Stonestar because of Anno Domini. One hundred and thirty miles from York, a ten–roomed 'cottage' to maintain and keep clean – an era had run its course.

★　　★　　★

It was with great concern that in 1988 I learned that the Railway Convalescent Homes had been deserted by the Transport Hospital Fund, for many years staunch and trusted partners. The two organisations joined hands in 1923, the one complementing the other, the RCH being a railway charity and the LMS Hospital Fund, as it then was, a Friendly Society. In 1968 the LMS Fund became the Transport Hospital Fund, extending its activities throughout British Railways, and I was proud to become the first signatory life member of that new fund which was to continue its close relationship with the convalescent homes. I approved of its work amongst railway staff and its welfare content, and still do. I was already a trustee of the RCH, and on the new fund being launched I helped to extend its membership, formerly confined to the LMS, to the North Eastern Region.

Imagine my dismay when I learned that the 'friendly' society had withdrawn its affiliation with the RCH on what appeared to be matters which I believe may have been reconciled easily if right and reasonable attitudes had been adopted. The THF withdrew its support entirely, directing its members seeking convalescence to homes outside the railway charity, denying in some cases their members who still wanted to use RCH centres their hospital cash allowance, and discarded unilaterally its connection with Transcare, a subsidiary which was described as a 'marketing organisation supported jointly by the Homes and the Hospital Fund which would offer to its contributors a comprehensive range of benefits covering all the benefits of the Hospital Fund together with membership of the Railway Convalescent Homes.' This therefore was a major upheaval in the voluntary 'caring' field.

One can only question the motives, however reluctantly, of the THF in taking the steps they have. With great publicity they have purchased a property, converting it to a 'Dallas'-type convalescent home, costing millions of pounds, in Dawlish of all places, where the RCH already have a splendid centre. Where is the logic of such spending? Why is it necessary to duplicate facilities, costing over TWO MILLION POUNDS*, with luxury accommodation for only 36 people? For a fraction of that amount, and with the proper community approach, I consider that improvements could have been made if necessary to existing homes over a much wider field.

For the THF to provide the same number of beds as available in the RCH, which even then would not satisfy every peak need, and to relate the cost of that, pro rata, to their Dawlish cost of £2m, would mean a total outlay of some £5.6m, followed by the high cost of running those centres. Bearing in mind these astronomical figures, I do appeal to the senior railway officers and their colleagues on the THF management body, who made the move to break with the RCH, to reconsider the position with the RCH trustees and try to find means of reconciliation. Surely in the situation where funds are voluntarily contributed from a common source – ie railwaymen and railwaywomen from all grades on British Rail – for what is an integral and complimentary element in staff welfare, a solution can be found with a common sense financial development of facilities, satisfactory to all.

I must declare my interest and say that I am a Vice President of the RCH as well as being a Life Member of the THF. I have had no formal discussion with either of the interested parties and must make it clear that the opinions I have expressed are my own personal views.

Meanwhile, I have admired the dignity by which the Chairman and Board of Trustees of the RCH have conducted the transitional arrangements in a difficult

*Railnews August 1990

situation. Also I pay tribute to Jim Cranswick BEM JP, long associated with THF at top level, who resigned from that body because he disagreed with their action, which he was quite entitled to do. It is equally appropriate to congratulate Valerie Sheridan of RCH staff, a mainspring in the development of Transcare, as a shining example of loyalty to her cause.

Meanwhile I stand by and watch with great disillusionment the morality and ethical standards of present-day activities, in this so-called caring field.

★　　★　　★

On leaving the service in 1969 I wished to keep in touch with colleagues who had also retired, and joined the Retired Railway Officers' Society in that year. We meet monthly in London, except in April when we gather in the Board Room in York. The Society's motto is:

'A man, Sir, should keep his friendship in constant repair.' *(Dr Johnson)*
– a sentiment, I am sure, we all endorse. I was President of this Society in 1981, when I broke with former routine and invited a railway union chief, Sidney Weighell, General Secretary of the NUR, to speak to us. During the same year I organised a meeting which I chaired in the Friends' Meeting House, London, inviting Sir Henry Johnson (the former Chairman, BRB, representing retired officers), Sir Peter Parker (then the current Chairman, BRB), Sidney Weighell (NUR) and Tom Jenkins (TSSA). Ray Buckton (ASLEF) was also invited, but did not accept, to join in a debate and commentary on topical railway subject. Could we, I thought, for once see all concerned with the future of railways meet together on one platform with a unified purpose? Nice thought! Anyhow, it was very well attended and a good try. See Appendix B for the report by *Railnews*.

I had also taken on the writing of a column in *Railnews*, headed 'The Old Guard' – again see Appendix B for extracts on topical subjects. In this column I endeavoured for three years to comment on the 'doings' of retired rail staff and especially on matters concerning pension bodies and the British Transport Superannuitants' Federation. Some comments from my first leader are reproduced below, since they are as relevant today as they were then:

> It is gratifying to us in retirement from long service with the railways to know that *Railnews* has allocated space for our news and comment.
>
> Our loyalties to the industry remain and in fact should be expressed, and the avenue is now open to us.
>
> Interest in the activities of our colleagues who are now taking the 'flak' in very difficult circumstances must inevitably continue when anything up to 50 years of one's life has been invested in the service.
>
> Members of the York branch of the British Transport Superannuitants' Federation have already expressed in open meeting that they want to keep in touch with current happenings on BR and express their best wishes.
>
> They naturally want BR to succeed and achieve the highest prestige. Just because we have retired doesn't mean we have 'folded up' and in

any case, to be absolutely selfish, let us admit we have a vested interest in the success of BR. So thank you *Railnews*.

I tried and tried to bring about representation of retired staff on the Joint Working Party of the Superannuation Funds, especially when concerned with the distribution of surplus funds, but without success. I consider it unworthy of our industry that former employees, who are now approaching a majority over 'active' staff, are excluded from having a direct say in how surplus funds, to which pensioners have contributed at a crucial time for investment, should be distributed. We have not requested 'trusteeship', we merely ask that as responsible employers British Rail should follow in a tangible way the hope of the Occupational Pensions Board in their report published on 1 February 1989:

> 'that employers and trustee bodies will become increasingly aware of scheme pensioners as a source of the knowledge, conscientiousness and independence of judgement which trustees require.'

I would hope that the unions represented on the working party, in their desire for 'fair play', would go along with that view.

★ ★ ★

In 21 years of retirement, with all its activities, its adventures and extensive world travel, I have enjoyed my new liberty. My wife and I have taken in the Canadian prairies, and the Rockies with their sock-eye salmon and friendly brown bears, mountain peaks and glaciers; seen the sunrise from the summits of the Italian Alps and the sunsets over Kerry; read by the midnight sun while sailing beyond the Arctic Circle and the North Cape; thrilled at the sunrise on Grand Canyon and the might of Niagara Falls; visited the Air Space Centre in Houston as special guests; perched on a camel in the African Desert; been in the remoter places on safari in New Zealand (including Hicks' Bay) and flown over the central deserts of Australia when they were in full bloom (only once in a hundred years does this bloom occur); taken lunch in a floating restaurant in Hong Kong and stood on the bridge over the River Kwai; been garlanded with flowers in Tahiti and nearly 'floored' by an outsize coconut falling from a tree on an out-island off Fiji; experienced a touch of Miami vice(!) and marvelled at the mysteries of the Everglades.

Even the warm Caribbean, the Canary Islands and Madeira have seen us. These and more have added to our previous travel experiences across Europe during my working years – to say nothing of having fished for trout and salmon in Scotland below the crags where eagles nest, or having walked through the valley in Wales from Capel Curig to Beddgelert when the dwarf rhododendrons were in full bloom.

But to return finally to 'my railway', in the 70 years since I joined the North Eastern Railway I have seen a fantastic transformation in the transport world, with the origination and development of road and air services striking hard against the railways, following generations of 'status quo'.

Early in the century the railway presence built up some industrial centres and dormitory areas, their traffic was at a high level, and their progress without serious threat. But when the petrol-driven vehicle arrived, things began to shift to their disadvantage. I saw the private car, the rapid growth of bus travel, and the freight road haulage element gain ground, infiltrating at all levels, initiating new thinking on the railways as to how to develop rail facilities, or on the other hand how to cut existing costs. This momentum was evident until the Second World War reversed the trend, and every sinew was strained to promote the war effort, cost or no cost.

Excluding that war period, therefore, I see a background of recurring periods of cost-cutting, economy here, economy there, cheered only by those more constructive periods, some of which have been outlined in this book, and not the luck of the person in a highly profitable and expanding business. Being for most of my career in the operating department – a big spender – this cost-cutting was obviously ever present, and one's credibility, one's standing, was so often measured by one's ability to achieve in that direction.

This situation had an effect on staff, and in the late 1920s and early 1930s many of my colleagues left the service during that period of the doldrums. Again following the end of the war, many 'high-flyers' left to join the steel companies, the Coal Board, and other industries where 'the grass was greener', and it was common thinking that passenger traffic would disappear from rail and there would be a serious fall in freight. I do not remember anyone forecasting that passenger traffic, especially main line business, would develop anything like it has done, as the development of motorways and airways was so potentially competitive. Certainly the Modernisation Plan of 1954 brought some sign of optimism and to me personally provided a happy hunting ground since it directly brought new and invigorating prospects to the operating function. It was a tonic, but as it got into its stride, along came yet another shake-up in the form of the 'Reshaping' report, widely regarded in the 'field' as a killer, with one or two sweeteners.

With it came a deluge of branch line closures involving a mass of consultations, both with the staff and the public. Running the railway became but a small part of the day's work as the greater urgency lay in destroying much of it and dealing with the considerable opposition from all sides 'out there' and from the unions 'inside'. Further, costings were revealing the unprofitability of specific freight traffics which resulted in curtailment of freight train services, which had a domino effect, on the reduction in marshalling yards and motive power depots, the smaller ones in both categories (usually the most efficient in their own function) going out first, all resulting in withdrawal and non-replacement of locomotives and rolling-stock. The Beeching era had arrived!

Amongst the negatives were some positives. The 'freightliner' scheme – oh, how bright the prospect! And where is it now? There was also the electrification of some trunk routes, notably on the LM Region, so not directly affecting the North East, and the development of high-speed diesel-hauled passenger trains. Ideas embodied in the APT buoyed up hopes for better performance but after its extensive trials it fell by the wayside. The 'Intercity 125' High Speed Trains have, however, been successful, and the trunk services are doing reasonably well. We in the North East now look forward to that dream of the past – electrification – coming true; it will be the climax for many of us who for 40 years have aspired towards it.

Of the 'star' locomotives, I saw the transition from the first 'Gresley Pacifics' and the silver streamliners (my favourite moment), to the elimination of steam, to the 'Deltics' on the East Coast route, the '125s', the design of which I greatly admire, and shortly the '225s'.

So, in completing this story I come to expressing my deep sense of loyalty and enthusiasm for 'my railway'. Not as an inanimate object, but as something alive and real. The locomotive expressing power, the station with its activity and bustle, the train, the signal box and signals, the running lines and layout. Its mood, its temper and its posture – striving, writhing, crowing, labouring, defying, comforting, powerful, lame, important, shining, dirty, mutilated, neglected, proud, submissive, praised, cursed – what other industry has had in turn so many facets? All these create an atmosphere which colours or emphasises my relationship with my railway, which apart from it having been my constant companion for a very long time, symbolises 'going places' and the attendant romanticism.

Today I continue to turn a lingering eye on what is happening right now over those still bright metals, with continuing pride in those things which are done well, perhaps occasionally raising a critical eyebrow. All this has made my railway connection worthwhile. I am proud of having been a 'North Eastern' man.

EPILOGUE: THE MAP

'This map shows the system operated by the former North Eastern Railway Company. In 1923 the company became part of the London and North Eastern Railway and in 1948 part of British Rail.'

A once white tiled map of the North Eastern Railway – described in its caption as a 'Historical Map 1900' – is fixed to the wall in York station opposite W. H. Smith's bookstall. It was already fixed there when I joined the service, it survived the air raids of the Second World War and the destruction which took place when the station was bombed, and it also escaped the threats from modernisation to remove it. Certainly it has been repaired and patched, but it is, so far as I am concerned, one of our greatest remaining perceptible railway treasures from the past. It shows the lines operated by the North Eastern Railway before its amalgamation with other railways to form the London & North Eastern, and for me it was a first lesson in NER geography, creating and engendering at the same time a loyalty which has remained constant ever since.

I first noticed this unusual structure when I started to commute to York headquarters. When I understood what it represented I became fascinated with it. It portrayed in bold outline, coloured yellow, the running lines from Shaftholme Junction, just north of Doncaster, in the south, to Berwick in the north, continuing its picture to Edinburgh, Glasgow and Inverness (in lines of a different colour) as if not wanting to exclude its Northern neighbour. Its eastern border was the North Sea, its western limits Leeds and further north the Pennines. I studied it, traced its main lines with my fingers, thumbed the main stations and wondered what they held. I had not visited them – they were just blobs on the map. I sought out the stations I knew and had worked at, Brafferton, Boroughbridge, Bainton, Foggathorpe, and the lines and places of which I had some knowledge. This map really had some significance – one could relate geography to actual places. It also gave significance to the immense business, with all its ramifications, carried out by the railway which I had joined.

Moreover, it conveyed to me a realisation of the wide expanse, the broad acres, of Yorkshire served by my railway, its branch lines wriggling away to remote places.

Places on the moors, on the wolds, in the vales, in the dales, and away to 'foreign' parts! Industrial areas and densely populated towns, and over to the west to Ilkley, to Garsdale, to Penrith across Stainmore, and to Carlisle. And all this was sustained by the backbone of the East Coast Main Line, which threw its branches eastward to Hull, to seaside resorts up the coast, and to the ironmasters' centres on Tees-side, Wearside and Tyneside. It featured inserts of the Tyne, Tees, Hartlepool and Hull areas, vital dock and industrial landmarks. Its large-scale presentation (74 in by 70 in) was easy to read. It was even drawn to scale!

If I heard a station name I had to trace it on this map, noting the branch on which it was located. I had heard that if a station clerk committed a misdemeanour, he was dispatched to the Hawes branch, a most remote area, to cool his heels. This had its joys for some, but retribution for recalcitrants! Where was this on the map? Renowned also was the blockage of Stainmore on the Penrith branch by snow. Where was Stainmore? The map, located where it was, allowed one to stand and stare.

Not only does the map show the North Eastern lines in yellow, but also other lines over which 'running powers' were in operation, shown by dotted yellow lines. Other railways – in black – the 'foreigners' – stretch down to Sheffield, across to Manchester and the west coast of Lancashire, to the Lake District, with certain lakes identified, Cumberland, and north to Scotland. For added interest it shows many mountains such as Ingleborough and Whernside. And what a sense of 'environment'. Cathedrals, Castles, Abbeys, Parks, Rivers, Battlefields, an education for anyone, are all indicated by different signs on this famous map of a famous railway. Do not let anybody destroy it! Besmirch it! Cast it aside because it is out-of-date and of no practical use! Let us have a specific preservation order placed on it! It was once covered by advertising material and, I suppose, written off as 'out-of-date', but is now resurrected.

Why I am so emphatic about its preservation is because in my experience I know there are people around who, in their enthusiasm, overlook the environmental aspects of (in their minds) a non-useful tool. I well remember one instance which at the time caused me dismay. It was concerned with a plan which someone produced – I think it was York City Council – for a new road to cross the River Ouse in York (this was before Clifton Bridge was built). The road was to diverge from the Tadcaster Road on the Mount, where even some of the Georgian property was at risk, was to cross the property adjacent to the Railway Institute, demolishing Queen Street bridge (always a problem), through the Station Hotel gardens, over the river, touching the Museum Gardens, to join Bootham. Railway working was also involved as running lines for coaching stock storage and other uses were to be eliminated, so I was called in to the discussions.

I was alarmed at the implications – not railway-wise, but amenity-wise – and to crown all one of my own senior colleagues seriously, and I mean seriously, suggested that the corner of the city walls opposite the Railway Institute should be taken down and placed further back to allow the road through! I cite this example to demonstrate how some minds work. That plan, which was, of course, discarded, ought to be dug out, if it still exists in the City Council archives, placed in a gilt frame and exhibited as a specimen of man's ingenuity.

So, future generations, watch this map, and treasure it as I do – that was, after all, my railway.

TAILPIECE

An extract from one of the most important publications in an Operating Officer's curriculum, the General Superintendent's issue of the 'Appendix to Working Timetable and Rule Book' for 1922, in the list of General Instructions, General Rule 22:

REMOVAL OF EGGS FROM CRATES ETC IN TRANSIT CONTAINING LIVE POULTRY

The attention of the staff is drawn to the fact that eggs found in crates etc containing live poultry must not under any circumstances be removed, but must be allowed to remain.

APPENDIX A

'THE PROSPECT OF DIESEL RAIL-CAR OPERATION IN THE NORTH EASTERN REGION'

A paper read by the author before The Newcastle Graduate and Student Society of the Institute of Transport, 25 October 1955.

The urgency for securing a cheaper method of traction has grown with the development of the internal combustion engine which revolutionised road transport. Much passenger traffic has passed to road transport, either to public services or to private car, and while public travel has increased enormously, rail has not obtained anything like a proportionate share of the general increase. The increasing cost of railway operation which jumped forward after World War II, and the growing availability of private cars and buses, made imperative a close study of conditions in this country with a view to introducing units operating at considerably lower costs than the orthodox steam train. Services worked by outmoded ponderous coaching stock and heavy engines are highly expensive to work; maintenance, preparation, and movement of steam engines is cumbrous. It was only natural, therefore, to investigate the possibilities of self-contained diesel-operated units, since diesel engines had proved themselves in road transport, and on railways in many parts of the world.

Many experiments had been made in an effort to reduce operating costs, and in the North Eastern we had seen tests with Sentinel cars and, to a limited extent, with diesel cars. The Western Region made prolonged diesel tests.

In 1951 an all-line enquiry was started to investigate the possibilities of introducing diesel rail units in this country. Conditions vary considerably, of course, in different parts of the world and one of the important factors which had to be borne in mind in Britain was the effect on the national economy of any proposal involving the increased use of imported oil and the decreased use

121

of coal, which up to recent years has been not only our natural source of power but also our cheapest form of fuel. Now oil is cheaper to import than coal!

Information made available through the Research Information Division of the British Transport Commission was reviewed, and discussion took place with railway officers with experience, including those of the Ulster Transport Authority and the Great Northern Railway of Ireland. Visits were made to Belgium, France and Germany where valuable information was obtained. France for example, has been one of the principal users of diesel traction over a long period where, in addition to running local services, a number of fast schedules are operated between some of the more important centres of population where electrification has not yet been carried out or traffic is too thin to justify electric traction. Experiences in Belgium and Germany have demonstrated the advantages of diesel operation over steam, both in operating facility and economy, while Holland has adopted this form of traction on a wide scale. The Ulster Transport Authority, which have made notable progress with diesel cars during the last few years, have been able to show considerable savings from the introduction of diesel units.

After considering all the evidence, therefore, it was decided to go ahead with diesel multiple-unit operation in this country for certain secondary services – trunk lines to be dealt with separately, worked either by electric traction or by diesel locomotives – with the possibility of using multiple units for some express services if found desirable and practicable.

Pros and Cons

In coming to this conclusion, it was necessary carefully to consider the advantages and disadvantages which diesel traction would bring, and from the study of the subject the following operational advantages of diesel cars over steam units emerged:-

(1) Quick acceleration, contributing to improved timings.

(2) Good performance over gradients, facilitating faster overall schedules where curvatures permit.

(3) Either-end drive, facilitating quick turn-round and reducing station movements and platform occupation; easy manipulation during emergency workings, including diversions and reversing movements.

(4) Operation by one motorman and more congenial conditions in the cab.

(5) Greater service availability arising from the following factors:-

(a) Elimination of major items of servicing, eg fire-cleaning, coaling, watering. Some of the dirtiest and most unpleasant railway work is thereby eliminated.

(b) Reduction in preparation and disposal time.

(c) Simplification of depot working through avoidance of turning, yard movements, etc.

(d) Ability to run for several trips without servicing.

In addition to operational advantages, the diesel car is an attractive travelling unit to the public. Up-to-date coaches offer clean and pleasant travel with good observation. They are in line with modern ideas and have a strong psychological appeal, and much of the attraction is due to the complete break from traditional railway practice. This element is particularly important in view of the relatively high standard of design and comfort set by the private motor car and the modern passenger road vehicle. Furthermore, diesel traction is in line with the 'clean air' campaign.

Diesel units with their improved performance make possible speedier and more frequent services facilitating the introduction of interval time-tables which should as far as practicable be the basis of all local schedules. They can be run profitably at a lower level of traffic than steam, and the economies which spring from the issue are due to the following factors:-

(1) Running for long periods (subject to efficient maintenance) and avoidance of intermediate breaks in a turn of duty for servicing. This is reflected in increased daily mileages and, therefore, in decreased cost per mile, particularly in the case of intensive services.

(2) Saving in fuel consumption when standing, and lower cost per mile when running – as the price of coal moves higher the more pronounced does this factor count in favour of diesels.

(3) Operation without a second man in the cab.

(4) Reduction in servicing and preparation work at depots.

(5) Reduction in terminal time at dead-ended stations, thus economising in operating costs.

In considering the possibilities of introducing the diesel rail-cars, certain disadvantages had to be borne in mind. They have limited carrying capacity and power compared with the conventional steam engines and coaches, and difficulty can arise at peak periods. Limitations in respect of wayside shunting movements, separate freight trips, the meagre parcels and luggage accommodation provided, and restriction on haulage of horse boxes and other through vehicles, are disadvantages associated with diesel car operation.

A further point is that diesel cars require special maintenance, fuelling and servicing facilities, and can generally only be justified at centres at which a fleet of diesel cars is based or where they are able easily to reach such centres.

The capital cost of new diesel coaches is a formidable aspect of any dieselisation scheme since the diesel power coach (the smallest self-contained passenger carrying unit) costs at present about £15,000, and a trailer without engine £9,000. Incidentally, a road passenger bus costs in the region of £4,500. The additional life of a diesel rail-car compared with the road vehicle must, however, be taken into account and as quantity production is developed there may be a lowering of the rail vehicle costs, but these figures go to illustrate the difference in first cost of rail and road vehicles, respectively. It is true, of course, that it is not necessary, and in fact it is undesirable for railway units to be built to last 40/50 years as has been the case in the past; it would appear to be much better policy to plan shorter lives for rolling stock and modernise currently. The life of a bus is from 6 to 8 years, and an aeroplane even less.

All these considerations had to be taken into account in assessing the scope for introducing diesel trains, and it became evident that two main prospects offered – one which promised an increase in net revenue by the reduction of operating costs, and the other the development of additional traffic by improved facilities. Some lines offered both prospects; some one and not the other in sufficient volume; isolated areas offered neither.

Experimental Scheme

In reviewing the requirements of the Region it was found that secondary and branch line services fell broadly into three categories: (1) rural, (2) suburban and inter-urban, and (3) medium and long distance.

In looking round for a suitable area in the North Eastern Region in which to launch an experimental scheme, a number of conditions were thought desirable. There should be scope for testing the extent to which traffic could be developed by use of diesel cars. There should be at the same time a substantial economy in operation compared with the existing steam service, and there should be conditions under which the performance of diesel units would be fairly tested. Should the test be on a cross-country line; should it be truly rural serving country branches; or should it be in the heavily populated industrial West Riding?

In rural areas the appearance of diesel units would give rise to hope on some of the branch lines which appeared to be doomed. In this connexion care was necessary to counteract any idea that diesels on branch lines would in any case be a paying proposition. It must be strongly emphasised that dieselisation is not the panacea for all ills. It is a wrong assumption when diesels are lightly referred to as the solution to the branch line problem – so much depends on local circumstances, not least of which is the potential traffic in the area served. In many rural areas the traffic potential is insufficient to justify a railway service of any kind, and from the point of view of national economy comparison must be made between the cost of running diesel rail-cars and the corresponding road vehicles in order to arrive at a reasonable solution. Generally speaking, bus services in such areas are more frequent than trains, and many country railway stations are not suitably situated for the villages they are supposed to serve. Convenience to the passenger in these circumstances usually decides the mode of travel adopted, and with rising costs it is clear that the position is becoming worse with little scope for developing rural rail services. Many of the busier branch lines would benefit from a diesel service, but with lack of true costing figures on diesel performance under conditions associated with each branch there are no grounds for making a categorical statement. So much depends on the total population, the incidence of difficult roads, and the necessity for maintaining a feeder facility or a public utility service.

In the inter-urban or suburban areas quite different conditions had to be considered. Frequent and regular bus services cater adequately for heavy flows of traffic, giving to many passengers a door-to-door service. The 'travel by bus' habit has become firmly established, and a walk to the station might dissuade the traveller from using even a new diesel car. Would season ticket holders on a road service, the shopper, or the traveller bent on recreation be attracted in sufficient numbers to make a diesel operated train service a success? What would be the effect on freight train working in these busier areas, station capacity and so on?

Under the heading of medium and long distance services the 60-mile cross-country run, almost parallel with its rival route via road, from Newcastle to Carlisle was attractive, particularly when looking further ahead one could visualise through cross-country services from places such as Sunderland to the

Lake District, or possibly through to the Cumberland Coast. Would the longer distance traveller demonstrate a preference for rail travel if diesels were introduced on this line?

After due consideration, it was thought that the first service should be introduced between Leeds Central and Bradford Exchange (over the old GN route) with an extension to Harrogate. In other words, the inter-urban location was chosen by the NE and subsequently selected by the BTC from all Region's proposals for the first experiment. There was in the Bradford area a population of about 250,000 and in Leeds about half a million, while Harrogate offered some scope for the development of social and residential traffic. Existing traffic was light and the train service irregular. The route chosen was one with difficult gradients and curvatures. The operation of a steam service on a suitable interval basis would in any case be impossible owing to restricted terminal capacity, whereas the freedom which diesel unit working gives by 'either end' drive and quick acceleration, would permit of a fast and frequent service. Undoubtedly the route chosen was one which would severely test the mechanical performance of any diesel units provided. It was with these points in mind that the experiment was initiated.

Briefly the scheme was this; starting in the summer of 1954 by covering the lines (2 routes) between Bradford Exchange and Leeds Central over the old GN Railway, giving a half-hourly interval service with every other train throughout most of the day projected to Harrogate. The interval trains run mainly via Stanningley, with additional trips via Pudsey Greenside. The number of services between Leeds and Bradford was increased by 18 per week-day. The services between Leeds and Harrogate were additional. It will be seen, therefore, that the new scheme provided for a substantial increase in train mileage (at the rate of 70,000 miles per annum) but, nevertheless, was estimated to produce a considerable improvement in net revenue. This has been substantiated by accountancy reviews which have been made from time to time for non-stop trains between Leeds Central and Bradford Exchange over a distance of 9 miles 36 chains is 17 minutes in one direction and 16 minutes in the other – not an outstanding performance – but the aim is to make the journey time in both directions 15 minutes. The publicity value of being able to say 'Leeds to Bradford in a quarter-of-an-hour by diesel train' will be appreciated.

Eight twin-car sets composed of two power cars coupled together, each equipped with 2 x 125 hp Leyland engines giving 500 hp in total, were provided. The weight of the two vehicles forming the set was 54 tons, giving a high power/weight ratio to enable the sets to accelerate quickly and operate satisfactorily over the severe gradients. Each 2-car unit comprises:-

(1) A motor composite car 57ft 6ins long over body, seating 16 first and 53 second class passengers.

(2) A motor third brake also 57ft 6ins long, seating 61 second class passengers.

The total seating accommodation is thus 130 passengers.

The coach-type seats are comfortable and fitted either side of a centre gangway (2-3 aside), and they are so arranged that passengers can, by selection, sit facing or back to the engine.

The driving compartment in each unit is divided from the passenger accommodation by a large glass partition, through which most of the occupants of the forward (and rearward) seats can watch the track and signals, and at the front during daylight the driver's handling of the train. The composite car has lavatory accommodation, and the motor second brake a compartment for the guard, baggage and parcels. The two vehicles of each unit inter-communicate through the vestibule door corridor connexion similar to that provided in long-distance passenger stock. The two doorways on each side of each car give access to the passenger compartments with separate doors to the driving and guard's compartments.

A special feature of the design is the extensive use of light alloy metal. The body and under-frame of each car is fabricated as one unit, and to reduce condensation and noise the whole of the inside structure and the underside of the floor is sprayed with asbestos. A maximum speed of 62 miles per hour can be obtained and acceleration is good, even up the gradients. The interior colour scheme is attractive. The seats have frames of tubular steel and are trimmed in maroon moquette in the second class and blue uncut moquette in the first class. Baggage racks formed of light alloy tubes in square sections are provided on both sides, running the complete length of the compartment.

Two units can be coupled together provided the driving compartments are formed at each end of the train. With four cars coupled together up to eight diesel engines can be synchronised and controlled from either end. From either driving position the driver can stop or start each engine individually, the performance of each being indicated by instruments in the driver's compartment. Braking is by vacuum equipment with the conventional handbrake and 'dead man's' device.

The engines are basically similar to those used for road transport vehicles and are positioned horizontally under the coach floor. These engines are easily accessible from the side of the vehicle.

Hot-air heating of the cars is electrically operated and is of experimental design.

A rather detailed description of these units has been given to convey a broad idea of the lay-out and accommodation which can be provided in diesel cars. Variations and improvements are being effected as new designs come along. The daily mileage performed by the most intensively worked diagram in the service is over 300 miles, which gives some idea of the hard work done. The units go into Bradford Hammerton Street motive power depot for maintenance purposes, where a section of the steam shed has been enclosed and protected from smoke, and fuelling facilities provided alongside. There is also a fuelling plant at Bradford Exchange station. Major overhauls are carried out at Derby Works.

Unfortunately, a good deal of mechanical trouble has occurred with the cars due to the experimental nature of some of the equipment provided. The units are being modified in the light of experience, and the first results of this overhaul appear to be satisfactory.

Despite the mechanical difficulties which have at times inconvenienced passengers, the diesel trains are proving very popular with the travelling public and receipts have gone up something like 120 per cent compared with steam-service days. In this connexion it is only fair to point out that more trains are being run and fares have been made more competitive with road. During the summer week-ends the peak traffic has sometimes been more than the diesels could cope with and passengers have had to be turned away. It is difficult to cater for exceptional contingencies of this kind, and it would be uneconomic to provide a high level of equipment to meet them when at other times the vehicles would not be earning to the full or were idle altogether. An interesting development on the West Riding diesel service is the running of Sunday trains through to Knaresborough – these have drawn large crowds during the good weather. A new and important daily facility (made possible by the ease with which diesel units can reverse at Leeds Central) has been provided by the through service between Bradford and Harrogate via Leeds, a convenience which is much appreciated by the passengers concerned.

There are plans for extending this scheme which will be popular with the public once the services are under way. It is planned to provide services from Leeds and Bradford to Ilkley and northwards to Keighley and Skipton. Vigorous efforts will be made to reinfuse those local West Riding lines directly serving important centres of population with new life, as undoubtedly enormous scope exists.

Development

Following the declaration of policy by the British Transport Commission that steam was to disappear, the North Eastern Region decided to go all out for dieselisation of appropriate local services. It was necessary to decide priorities, and the next route which offered considerable scope was that from Newcastle to Middlesbrough covering the industrial Tyneside, Wearside and Tees-side areas.

Newcastle-Middlesbrough

Trade and industry in this area are expanding rapidly, and the three largest conurbations on the North East Coast will be served by this scheme; 'heavy' industry flourishes in the area side by side with a wide range of 'light' newcomers, many of which, while not producing much for the railways on the freight side, are potential sources of revenue from the passenger angle. The facilities for shopping and entertainment at Newcastle are a source of attraction to residents in the Tees-side and Wearside areas, and by the introduction of a good diesel service it is hoped to see a return to rail of those who travel by other means for business or pleasure between these large centres of population.

The conditions associated with this scheme are different from those of the West Riding in that the traffic to be catered for is longer distance, heavier, and embraces a good deal of intermediate travel. Larger trains are required. Against the 2-coach units in the West Riding, 4-coach trains are required on the Newcastle-Middlesbrough line for the majority of services and the first scheme for this route has been planned to cater accordingly. It was decided that the most heavily loaded trains would go over to diesel working later, in the form of 6-coach trains. The type of unit for stage 1 is of 4-car design consisting of 2 power-cars each fitted with two 150 hp engines and two trailers. It will be noted that engines of higher horse power than those supplied to the West Riding units will be provided. The seating for 20 first class and 206 second class passengers will be arranged two on each side of the central gangway of each coach and will differ from the West Riding arrangements of two seats at one side and three on the other side of the gangway, thus giving extra room to the passenger for the longer average journey. The attractive interior decoration with bright contrasting colours strikes a new note in railway design.

The units will be run on an hourly interval basis and the fleet will be scheduled to cover about 80,000 miles per annum more than the existing steam mileage. The power/weight ratio will be 6 to 1 and the journey time will be reduced by 12 to 22 minutes on the throughout run between Newcastle and Middlesbrough.

Deliveries of the units started in September and they entered regular service on Monday, November 21st. These are the first 4-car multiple unit trains to be operated in this country. In fact on certain services eight cars will run coupled together as one train – also the first train of this size to be run to regular schedule.

A natural sequence to the Newcastle-Middlesbrough scheme is one covering the Newcastle-Carlisle line. The type of unit to be used over this route is somewhat similar to that on the Newcastle-Middlesbrough, and it is hoped that through working will eventually be arranged from Tees-side to Carlisle and possibly further West, since through coaches are such an important feature to passengers when choosing their mode of transport. Inter-working of the vehicles may also help the operating problem at Newcastle (Central) Station. The Newcastle-Middlesbrough and Newcastle-Carlisle units will be maintained at Gosforth Car Sheds, where plans are being made to extend the present accommodation.

Hull

A different type of area was next explored, and it was considered that the Hull area offered scope for a scheme based on 2-car units with lower horse power and consequently lower running costs than those provided for the West Riding as the terrain is without heavy gradients. A number of services operate into dead-end stations, including Hull itself, which involves additional movements by steam locomotives in rounding trains, and the advantages of diesel unit operation in such cases are most pronounced. The units decided upon were similar to those which had been ordered by the Eastern Region for their Lincolnshire and Eastern Region for their Lincolnshire and Eastern Counties' schemes. The trains consist of two cars, one powered by two 150 hp engines and one driving trailer with 16ft van space. Thirteen sets are required to work stage 1 of the scheme. The services radiating from Hull will in the main serve branch lines where it cannot be hoped to develop a lot of new traffic but considerable saving in operating and other costs will be achieved. Even so, and taking into account the additional revenue which may be secured, it is doubtful whether the passenger train services on some of the branches will completely pay their way. This applies to many country branches, and only experience can show whether, by running carefully planned diesel services, these doubtful lines can contribute a reasonable revenue to the Commission's undertaking.

Further schemes

Further schemes, which are well advanced, cover the Darlington/Saltburn line – with off-shoots to Bishop Auckland and Richmond; County Durham lines catering for Newcastle/Sunderland, Sunderland/Bishop Auckland, Bishop Auckland/Newcastle and further North from Newcastle/Alnwick. Extension plans in the East and West Ridings are also well advanced. As new units are produced, improvements in fittings and equipment will be made with complete freedom of inter-change and coupling of vehicles. The Region as a whole should, within the next three years or so, be fairly well equipped with multiple diesel units as there are 542 cars (271 motor, 271 trailer) on order and allocated to the North Eastern Region for delivery within that period. Roughly speaking, this represents a capital expenditure of £6 million.

Maintenance

With a fleet of cars of this size involving such large scale capital investment, it is evident that the equipment must be well looked after and the question of maintenance in all its aspects must receive the utmost attention right from the start. A well-trained technical staff, with adequate facilities, should be available, and the development plans must provide accordingly. It would be a mistake to neglect in any way, or regard as of secondary importance, the maintenance aspect either from the point of view of intermediate maintenance or main overhaul.

Depots adequately equipped will be placed strategically so that operating movement is reduced to the minimum, and at points which favour the economical diagramming of trainmen and units. Obviously, however, first cost of new depots must be weighed against existing facilities and available sites. Proposals in the North Eastern Region so far provide for depots at Bradford, Newcastle, Darlington and Hull.

A structure providing inspection pits, including side pits, and overhead travelling crane, with cleaning facilities and re-fuelling plant adjacent, will be the sort of thing required. The usual offices, stores and small shops must, of course, be part of a plan for a running shop equipped to deal with servicing and maintenance. Cleanliness and adequate lighting are of great importance, while appropriate heating in the workshops is necessary, having in mind the intricate work of fitters. Of necessity the conception of a diesel maintenance depot differs fundamentally from the traditional type of locomotive running shed and, in general, very few of the existing steam running shed facilities can be used. The whole maintenance staff approach will have to be guided to a routine inspection based on preventive maintenance, more detailed than that normally accorded to the steam locomotive because the mechanism is more complex.

In view of the great mechanical complexities of diesel maintenance and the need to reap full advantage of the higher availability hoped for under diesel traction working, maintenance on the basis to engine replacement for major overhaul or defect is a practical necessity and plans will be made accordingly. All engines on multiple-unit cars will, for major repair or examination, be removed from the vehicles and sent to main shops for attention. Major overhaul depots will have to be provided in various parts of the country – number and location will depend on how successful diesel operation is, to what extent it expands and, of course, to what extent the diesel locomotive and main line electrification are adopted.

Training

A most important point on the maintenance side is the training of technical staff. An efficient body of fitters, electricians and other technical people, including drivers, is an integral part of any diesel scheme and there may be some difficulty during the transitional period in building up a competent team at each centre, with all that the new technique demands. Training is being encouraged, both through training schools and in practical work; the more knowledge which can be imparted to the ground staff and the more efficient the routine applied to maintenance matters, the greater success will attend diesel operation.

A new school for the training of motive power staff in the operation and maintenance of diesel traction units was opened at Derby in July. At this school, the first of its kind on British Railways, it is intended initially that staff from all the Regions shall be eligible to attend fortnightly intensive courses of instruction. Other schools will undoubtedly be necessary in the future.

Costs

As intimated earlier in the paper, it is evident that the cost of operating diesel units will vary on different sections of line and in different parts of the country. Line conditions in hill areas call for very different effort and performance from those in flat terrain, while the structure of the time-table worked influences the diagrammed mileage per unit; furthermore, different types of diesel trains made up of two, three or more cars per train, will be employed according to demands. It will be misleading, therefore, to quote actual operating costs for any particular service at this stage as being typical. Evidence forthcoming from experience we have already had shows that, broadly speaking, the cost per train-mile for diesel units, i.e. wages, fuel, cleaning, maintenance and renewal, is roughly half that of the steam services displaced. In the West Riding to date the cost of operation is rather higher than half the steam cost but this is largely because of the teething troubles experienced with an experimental scheme. Data is being collected throughout the country which will help in costing more accurately existing and proposed diesel schemes, and it may be that with experience in production and operation, further substantial economies not yet confirmed will be achieved from a switch over to this form of traction.

A point which has to be considered in assessing the financial value of a scheme is the number of spare vehicles which have to be bought and maintained to release units for maintenance purposes, to insure against failure, and to cater for peak traffics. Spare cover for maintenance and emergency may be to the order of 20 or 30 per cent according to the size of the fleet – experience in Holland where diesel multiple unit working has been widely adopted has settled this figure at round about 20 per cent. The provision of spares for additional peak traffics requires careful thought. The peak problem is a difficult one to solve even with steam trains where there is a substantial margin for moving extra traffic both in respect of motive power and accommodation. The position will no doubt arise, therefore, if we are to keep our costs down, where on busy lines at certain periods of the day, or during certain seasons of the year, some standing of passengers will have to be tolerated. That is nothing new on suburban routes, be they rail or road. It comes down to this, that it is patently uneconomic to provide in all cases the full quota of seats for a spasmodic upsurge of short-term traffic. While ordinary spare steam stock remains available there will be an outlet for major peak demands by using steam engines and sets to work the surplus traffic, and it will in fact be necessary for many years ahead to live with both diesel and steam during peak periods over routes which ordinarily have been turned over to diesel operation. Later, when the steam locomotive disappears, diesel locomotives hauling ordinary coaches will no doubt have to fulfil the role of the relief train. A certain amount of juggling with the rail-cars will presumably be possible so that summer peaks on less important lines can be covered by transfer of multiple-unit sets from secondary main lines; the removal of the sets from the secondary main lines will then be met by providing trains worked by a separate motive power unit.

Great opportunities will arise for operating special excursions and tours such as the London Midland Region have demonstrated this summer by using their 'Cumberland' units for tours of the Lake District. The use of a complete unit by an organised party which can be worked through difficult junctions and operated over rural routes must open up an attractive vista to passenger sales representatives without causing severe headaches to train-timing staff.

Further Prospects

Having described the immediate prospect of diesel rail-car operation in the North Eastern Region, it is interesting to consider what is likely to take shape in the longer term. The nearest prospect is of higher powered diesel units working some of the long-distance important cross-country trains, and in this connexion Leeds to Manchester and Liverpool services will be among those to receive early consideration. Hull to Liverpool will also be to the forefront when thought might be given to a fast diesel express, East to West, linking three major ports with a named train – say 'The Humber-Mersey Express'. We can imagine present difficult cross-country journeys, involving reversing en route, being made with comparative operating ease without those movements and station working problems associated with engine changing. On the Continent experiments are being made with international diesel trains and with fast businessmen's services – out from the province to the capital in the morning and back at night, and in Ireland there are inter-city expresses between Belfast and Dublin.

Experiments will take place with horizontal underslung engines of considerable horse power and the results will be compared with other types of diesel traction. In this connexion there are bound to be opinions in favour of diesel locomotives on the one hand, and multiple unit under-floor engines on the other. There will also be opinions about the provision of a separate engine compartment containing the higher powered vertical type of engines. The pros and cons are very largely on technical points and stray away from the main object of this paper. There will be views on retaining steam power and steam diehards will fight a strong rearguard action. We must, however, be progressive, and the change-over ·s indeed a challenge to steam engineers, in particular a challenge to the men who will drive and maintain the units under such different conditions from those to which they have been accustomed. It will be interesting and rewarding work, and there can be no doubt that they will meet this challenge successfully.

Apart from the motive power angle (and no aspect can exert such a direct influence on transport as the modernisation of motive power) there is a future for train and coach design which should not be lacking in progressiveness. There is a need to capture the imagination of the public by giving a 'modern' touch to our diesel trains. We must in fact adopt a modern conception of transport design such as the aircraft and motor industries have so emphatically done, and flourished because of it. It is important that we should search for something which will appeal without offending good taste, both inside the coaches and outside, and whether we think they should be streamlined or square-ended, a policy should be adopted which produces refreshing and attractive results.

Developments of the future may provide long-distance multiple units, air-conditioned, with reclining seats and other luxury appointments which will compare favourably with facilities provided by air lines. We can no doubt look forward to much lighter weight units for operation on branch lines where the Guard will be a Conductor as well as Guard, and be able to issue tickets – and describe the scenery to the tourist. Alternatively, the entrance to the branch line car may be via the Driver, who would take fares as passengers enter the coach. All sorts of new departures will undoubtedly have to be considered if many of the local services are to compete successfully with road interests – which are not standing still!

APPENDIX B

'THE OLD GUARD'

These extracts from my monthly column in *Railnews* follow the introductory comments on page 114, and are given as representing some thoughts on issues current at the time of publication.

It was with regret that I ceased writing my column, but other pressures led me to relinquish the job. I had enjoyed it very much indeed, and hoped that someone else would take it on as I think the 'oldies' should have a voice through the medium of our staff newspaper.

SEPTEMBER 1981

THERE WAS a feeling of 'an occasion' when Sir Peter Parker attended a rally of retired railway staff in the Tempest Anderson Hall at York. Nearly 400 members of various bodies heard him give news of current affairs and future prospects.

The rally, initiated by York BTSF and supported by the RROS, also attracted a contingent from the North Eastern group of officers, York BRRSA, the NER Pension Society and individuals from many parts of the country. It provided a meeting ground for former colleagues and demonstrated their continuing interest in the railways.

It was hoped the event would encourage retired staff to join an active group to get advice as required, information regarding facilities available to retired staff and keep friendships 'in constant repair'.

Sir Peter said that the railways were entering a most difficult period. The future, however, was good but there were two priorities – improved productivity and long-term investment.

The electrification plan recently approved by the Government was an example of the sort of forward planning needed. Asked how retired people could help, Sir Peter said that more meetings of this kind could bring news and facts to the notice of those interested. Such events opened up new possibilities for retired staff to serve the whole railway community.

As chairman of the rally I told Sir Peter: 'We wish to convey to colleagues at all levels our goodwill and earnest hopes for a successful future. We are very proud of our railway heritage and we want the present and future railway to achieve the highest prestige. We particularly want to say that we share your concern over the present difficulties which you have described as grim and formidable, and we all wish you well.'

With Sir Peter were Board Member Cliff Rose and ER's Frank Paterson. Also present were Ernest Booth, national chairman of the BTSF; Frank Colley, chairman of the York branch of BRRSA; Tom Yellowley, chairman of the NER Pension Society; Fred Margetts, former Member of BR Board; and ER's former GM Derek Barrie.

On a personal note may I thank members who supported the event, particularly those who helped with the arrangements. In a letter to me Sir Peter says: 'Many thanks for a wonderful event – I found it an uplifting experience.'

OCTOBER 1981

MANY retired staff actively support the Railway Convalescent Homes and Railway Benevolent Institution by voluntarily giving their time and effort to help them survive.

Sir Peter Parker is president of both charities.

John Whitehouse has been chairman of the RCH Board of Trustees since he retired as Birmingham divisional staff officer in 1977. His administrative skill, with valuable assistance from fellow trustees, steered the RCH through difficult times to substantially improve the fund's financial position.

Many other retired BR staff up and down the country work hard for the homes to ensure their continuance.

There are four railway convalescent homes, all with a high standard of cuisine and facilities and equipped with colour television.

At Llandudno and Margate the homes take only women while the Dawlish and Ascog residences cater for men. Should husband and wife both need convalescence the man would go to Dawlish or Ascog, his wife to Llandudno or Margate. Married couples can only convalesce together at Ascog but one will be regarded as a paying patient at a special rate of £40 a week.

Wives are covered by their husbands' contributions and retired staff are eligible for five years after normal retirement if they have been direct contributors to the RCH, Transport Hospital Fund or Derby Day Centre Hospital Fund. No contributions are payable after retirement and no charges are made curing this five-year period.

PT identity card holders can get free BR tickets from their homes to the station nearest the convalescent home and a free taxi meets the trains.

The Railway Benevolent Institution caters for the young and elderly, widows and orphans – in short, those in need. These two railway charities, together with the welfare organisation, cover the whole spectrum of help and advice available.

There is a home for the Aged at Dorking which may be of interest to widows and widowers seeking security in later life.

As with many similar funds the RBI management are always seeking new ways to improve their financial position and welcome new members from among active staff.

On the board of management of this important charity, of which part-time BR Board Member Sir Robert Lawrence is chairman, are many retired railway officers who devote time to furthering and developing the interests of the constituents of the RBI, St Christopher's Railway Children's Home at Derby and the Dorking home known as Boxhurst.

NOVEMBER 1981

GUEST speaker Sidney Weighell, NUR general secretary, brought out the enormous problems facing BR because of financial limitations when he addressed the Retired Railway Officers' Society.

His thought-provoking review of past upheavals highlighted the hot and cold approach to railway social and industrial needs by successive governments and the time and effort wasted by management and staff on re-organisation instead of concentrating on running the railways.

Comparing the financial support many foreign railways have from their national funds, and their attitudes to railways as compared with this country, Mr Weighell called for strong action to get long-term policies agreed and decisions taken to save an otherwise wasting asset. As an example he cited the 3,000 track miles which are without adequate finance for necessary renewal.

Former BR chairman Sir Henry Johnson supported Mr Weighell's main points. Like many others he too had experienced the frustrations of ever-changing transport policies and national motives.

Sidney Weighell is a third-generation trade union official. Former officers in the audience referred in complimentary terms to his late father who was a signalman at Northallerton and general secretary of the former NE Regional Sectional Council No 3 (staff side).

I have been given some details of the activities of the BRRSA in York. The extra 'R' is for 'retired'. It is a self-governing body within BRSA, operating as a section of the local BRSA branch. Members meet in the clubhouse and participate in other branch activities. Fees are small.

The BRRSA have their own social programmes, catering arrangements, a newsletter, outings, and Christmas party. Secretary, Peter Collins, 94 Cranbrook Road, York YO2 5JH, has details. Other retired staff who work for this branch are Bert Harriman and Burt Neilson, vice-presidents, chairman Frank Colley and Norman Haigh, treasurer.

NOVEMBER 1982

EVERY month a number of retired North Eastern Region officers make their way to Darlington where they gather for a 'natter' and lunch. This has been going on for many years and apparently loses none of its attractions. Old colleagues discuss old colleagues and recount the good old days. Do they remember Jack Richardson, Low Sproat, Frank Petty and others like them?

There is one former district motive power superintendent who is still going strong – Ron Taylor who ruled at Leeds with strong, benevolent effect. Another Taylor – George – former C&W engineer at Doncaster and fast approaching the age of 90, turns up to make his contribution along with Edward Triffitt (ex-CCE) and ex-Board member Fred Margetts, who probably will argue with Harold Hoyle, former rolling stock manager at the Board.

Resolutely keeping the pot boiling is Ted McClelland (ex-DOS, Middlesbrough) who valiantly acts as secretary, while Ben Coulson is this year's chairman.

Another member, Frank Jagger (ex-director of establishment, BRB) has a flair for cycling and one can often see him, in suitable garb, either dismantling or putting together his bicycle before or after train travel. He writes:

'When the shaking down process of retirement was accomplished I began to make use of my pedigree bicycle. Once a week (usually washing day) I take off for a day's outing, wet or fine, rain, snow or blow. With bicycle, a bob or two for a pint and a sandwich and a flying start from York, by mid-morning I can be anywhere between Carlisle and Cambridge, or Berwick and Burton-on-Trent, with time for a six hours' ride, and be home the same night. And two or three times a year I am off for a week's tour to remoter parts – Wales, Scotland, East Anglia or the West Country...

'How you may ask, do I cope with high-speed trains which will not take bicycles in the van? I have a special lightweight folding machine, made of aircraft alloy. It weighs only 20lbs, has a 4-speed gear, and folds so small it goes on the luggage rack. It intrigues the guards mightily.

'What a very lucky man I am, to travel leisurely through new country, on by-roads and country lanes, not knowing what is round the next corner or over the next hill, or where I shall take my next meal or where I shall sleep. To me it is paradise.'

★　★　★

The annual meeting of the northern section (ER) of the Railway Convalescent Homes in York attracted a number of retired members. ER's former management development officer, Allen Miller, was in the chair and a welcome guest was Miss Norah Pateman, former matron of the Herne Bay Home in Kent.

Reference to other former matrons was made and to the sterling service they gave to the homes – Miss Mai Moylan (Llandudno), Lady Benstead (Ascog), Miss Madalein Pages (Margate) and Miss Eileen Lamont (Dawlish). The homes, which provide a high standard of facilities in excellent locations, are embarking on a new and promising programme of activities, offering more facilities for all members and including retired couples (one of whom should have been member) who can comply with the relaxed conditions which are to apply.

FEBRUARY 1982

A CALL to Parliament for a stable, progressive and continuing national policy for Britain's railways will be the theme of a rally of retired staff on 6 April.

Former BR chairman Sir Henry Johnson will lead the debate, followed by Sir Peter Parker and supported by NUR general secretary Sidney Weighell and TSSA general secretary Tom Jenkins.

Venue will be the large hall of Friends' Meeting House, Euston Road, London – directly opposite Euston station and also well-placed for St Pancras and King's Cross stations.

Over the years BR has been subjected to changing political attitudes, frequently frustrating and destroying planning and development. It is hoped the rally will have countrywide appeal and draw attention to this ignominious situation.

Already the rally has the enthusiastic backing of BTSF and RROS officers. But I want to stress that the rally is open to all retired railwaymen and women. So put the date in your diary now and let's make it a 'house-full' event. There's room for 1,200.

★   ★   ★

Contributors to the North Eastern Cottage Homes & Benefit Fund are aware of the small, comfortable homes for retired railwaymen in various parts of the North-East. The fund has now become a registered housing association with several new building schemes in progress, including properties with accommodation for resident wardens.

A capital cost of £6 million is involved to provide sheltered accommodation spread over an area of 10,000 square miles from Berwick-on-Tweed in the north to a line from Hull-Selby-Leeds and West Yorkshire in the south.

Voluntary initiative and help from retired railway people has made a valuable contribution to the continuing expansion of the organisation. Ten retired staff sit on the management committee which is chaired by ER's former chief finance officer Tom Foster. The fund is administered from Darlington by Jim Forster and a staff of 12.

★   ★   ★

A campaign for the recruitment of more members has produced excellent results for the York branch of BTSF, a recent meeting was told.

The branch has unfortunately lost its secretary Burt Neilson for health reasons. His successor is Wilf Cooper, 31 Greenfield Park Drive, Stockton Lane, York YO3 0JB.

MARCH 1982

NEWS that all retired staff attending the London rally next month will be granted an extra free rail pass for the journey shows how seriously BR top management are treating the event.

Get your ticket through the usual channels but don't forget to mention that it is for return travel from your home station to the London rally and is *in addition* to your normal free-pass quota. It will be valid only on that day.

The rally – on Tuesday, 6 April at Friends' Meeting House, Euston Road – starts at 2pm.

Top people from active and retired sections of BR as well as the railway unions will meet on the same platform to emphasise the urgent need for a stable, progressive and continuing national policy for railways.

Leading the debate will be former BR chairman Sir Henry Johnson, followed by Sir Peter Parker and NUR general secretary Sidney Weighell and supported by TSSA general secretary Tom Jenkins.

The event is being sponsored in part by *Railnews*.

★ ★ ★

THE Old Comrades of the 156 Company (Southern Railway) Royal Engineers will meet in the BRSA premises, Waterloo station, at 12 noon on Friday, 30 April. The company was formed from personnel of the former Southern Railway and was mobilised with three other companies of railway staff in 1939. Members are keen to keep the reunion going.

★ ★ ★

MY term of office as president of the Retired Railway Officer's Society expired on 1 February and at the annual general meeting of the society members welcomed to the chair Mr John Read FCCA, former controller of finance, Shipping and International Services Division.

★ ★ ★

I HAVE been looking at the Golden Rail facilities available to retired staff for summer holidays, self-catering and spring short breaks. The summer short breaks brochure will be published shortly.

All staff entitled to BR free passes are offered reductions from the public price for all holidays featured. Holidays shown in the new Continental brochure are, however, excluded from the arrangement.

MAY 1982

A CALL to Parliament for a stable, progressive and continuing national policy for Britain's railways was made by former BR chairman Sir Henry Johnson when he addressed a *Railnews*-sponsored rally of retired railway staff in London last month.

'I believe a good, modern railway is essential for the country's future,' said Sir Henry.

'Over the years there has been a sad lack of transport policy as a whole and for railways in particular.

'There should be a consensus between the political parties so that railways are not subjected to continual changes of ministers and policies.'

The rally, at Friends Meeting House, Euston, was attended by about 300 retired railway men and women from many parts of the country.

Their aim in getting together was to reaffirm their support for BR in its present troubles.

Other speakers included Sir Peter Parker, Mr Sidney Weighell, NUR general secretary, and Mr Tom Jenkins, general secretary of the TSSA.

Sir Peter Parker told the gathering: 'We want a railway we can take pride in. We must look for consistency and commitment – a clear transport policy.

'Government must decide how much from the national purse should go to transport in general; how the cash should be divided between public and private transport and how it should be split up between the various forms of transport.

Referring to BR's Rail Policy document of 1981 he reiterated the Board's objectives – to provide railway services for the needs of industry and the public efficiently while keeping within the financial aims set by the Government.

He said the railways were facing a mountain of arrears in necessary expenditure. Even if the Government gave the go-ahead for electrification now the Board might not be able to implement it.

In strong, fighting mood Sidney Weighell said he had jumped at the chance to address the rally.

He attacked Government plans to cut back on funding and bitterly criticised the Board's statement concerning their 'confidence in management's ability to work towards the new cost constraints imposed upon them'.

'Such shackles imposed by Government cannot be tolerated.' declared Mr Weighell and warned that his union would fight 'tooth and nail' any attempts by the Board to cut costs by reducing funds allocated for wage rises.

He opposed plans to sell off hotels, shipping services and engineering workshops to private enterprise.

'Even the private rail bosses of the past – and I'd not much time for them – saw that it was necessary to own hotels, workshops, docks and ships if you wanted a consolidated transport industry.

'I don't ask for a featherbed for rail people – but we want a fair crack of the whip. In return we will give this country the finest railway in the world.

'But if there is no change of policy by 1983 there will be nothing left to fight for.'

Mr Jenkins warned the Board against taking panic measures.

'We want an integrated, publicly-owned transport system. But massive investment – not least electrification – is necessary.

'If we cannot have the largest option we should go for features of it.

'And Government should maintain an adequate PSO.'

Mr Jenkins told the former railway men and women at the rally they were in a good position to spread the gospel for BR to the general public.

'Having a little more time on your hands than serving colleagues I am sure you will try to get public support for our aims.'

ASLEF general secretary Ray Buckton had been invited to the rally but was unable to be there.

The national Press were represented in strength and many reports of the event appeared in the following day's papers as well as in independent railway broadcasts. I express my thanks to *Railnews* for helping to make it possible.

★   ★   ★

AT the recent four-monthly meeting of the British Transport Superannuitants' Federation in London it was reported that following a recruitment drive total membership had reached 20,606 with further increases expected from large-scale early retirements.

This splendid result was a reflection of the work done in the various branches, councils and associations of BTSF throughout the country with the co-operation of the BRB staff and the pensions office.

There was still plenty of room for improvement in membership and the results so far are a pointer to those who have not yet joined.

A pamphlet is to be distributed in November to BR Fund members already retired from organisations other than BR.

Retired staff (and widows of staff concerned) of NFC and Dock authorities are to be allowed an additional free pass per year, including 1982, on an ex-gratia basis, a concession greatly appreciated.

Those concerned are NCL and BT Dock Board, who at the time of transfer on 1.1.69 had completed 25 years or more railway service.

The NFC and BTDB have agreed in conjunction with BRB to administer the arrangements.

In another context it was reported that the Isle of Man Steam Packet has withdrawn the privilege ticket facility from NFC employees and pensioners. Further consideration will be given to this matter.

Chairman Ernest Booth supported by Fred Childs reported on their meeting with TSSA about the need for BTSF representation on the Superannuation Fund committee and JWP.

The Federation hold strong views on this and find it difficult to understand the TSSA's reluctance to agree.

When it is appreciated that matters such as the disposal of surpluses of the Old Funds (96 per cent of members are annuitants) and the effects of the 1980 Transport Act on supplementation are involved, the claim for representation is unanswerable.

To emphasise the position it should be noted that pensioners would shortly be the only people in the Old Funds yet they have no direct representation.

It is understood BRB would not object to a form of representation from BTSF.

It was hoped after further consideration that TSSA would accept and acknowledge the principle involved supported by facts which amply justify representation.

Reference was made to the Serpell Committee on the Review of Railway Finances which is now considering the future of railways. BTSF had, following an invitation to do so, submitted their views in a report to the Committee's secretary.

BRB's controller of corporate pensions John Goodchild gave a talk to the meeting on current pension matters. This was warmly welcomed.

Colin A. Grant (Formerly of Western Region) was appointed Hon secretary of the Federation in succession to Reg Wheeler who had held office for six years, and to whom appreciation for his services had previously been expressed.

JANUARY 1983

INCREDIBLE! That was how many senior retired railway officers expressed their feelings on the views of Mr Lance Ibbotson when he said on radio and elsewhere that the main suburban railway system should be superseded by road transport.

They found it hard to believe that a former general manager of the WR and SR, after investing a life's work and contributing so much to maintaining and developing the industry as it is today, and for which many have a great loyalty, could in retirement clobber its future so dramatically.

That he meant what he said was evident in the interview in radio's World at One and reference by the media has indicated considerable interest in the views of one so senior and experienced in the railway service.

Comment continues: 'Had Mr Ibbotson made constructive suggestions on the need for a more cohesive transport system rather than a total retreat from the railway function then that would have been applauded' – though of course the cynics would no doubt have cried 'old hat'. So, perhaps the shape, size and source of the proposal was intended to shake up thinking about railways.

But the proposal as at present expressed ignores certain realities and doesn't ring true of the author.

The facts about the economic value of disciplined bulk rail movements in this congested and built-up island speak loudly for themselves. And engineers have repeatedly said that disused rail tracks under consideration for road use often have inherent massive restrictive features, some of which are impossible to solve within acceptable conditions and costs. Unlike, for example, the position in USA where wide open spaces approaching and within main cities make road monopoly practicable.

It is hoped that the assessment and balancing of the options will be achieved quickly and that Parliament will seek to implement findings where we in retirement, as well as those in the service, can see the prospect in the future of a compact, dynamic, progressive and continuing railway system provided with the necessary resources, and enjoying the full and loyal support of the railway community.

AUGUST 1983

RAILWAY museums offer retired employees a feast of nostalgia.

Top of the 'pops' is, of course, the National Railway Museum at York visited by over a million enthusiasts a year. It's heart-warming experience to contemplate the care and professionalism which has been lavished on the collection and exhibition of such a magnificent show of items ranging from locomotives and station memorabilia to fascinating old documents.

Less well-known, perhaps, is Beamish open-air museum in Co Durham. Here an old NER passenger loco draws a vintage (circa 1900) 'compo' coach (no corridor) over a perimeter line, signalled by original semaphore signals overlooked by an old lever-equipped signalbox with tablet instrument.

The luxurious upholstery of the first-class carriage, complete with clerestory roof, exemplifies the scope given to the coach builders in those 'good old days'.

A replica of *Rocket* operates over a short section of the line and retired men can have a field day examining the steam pressure and working equipment 1825-style.

The sight of the former Rowley station with its Victorian fireplace, ticket racks, shuttered ticket window, oil-handlamp and single-needle morse telegraph instrument will evoke memories for any railwayman who started his working life at a small country station.

Yes, Beamish is the place for a good wallow in nostalgia.

OCTOBER 1983

MANY retired railwaymen who have met Sir Peter Parker and many who watched as onlookers of his work as chairman of BR feel considerable regret at his retirement.

There are those now retired, who have worked under his leadership and been inspired by him, and there are those who have just looked on who feel this way. Despite the inevitable critical eye of this retired 'onlooker' what I saw over Sir Peter's term of office was refreshing, notwithstanding the setbacks of such a hot seat.

Two years ago at a Retired Railway Officers' meeting, and at an enthusiastic gathering of members of BTSF & BRRSA, Sir Peter gave his reasons for accepting a further two years in the chair commenting on his hopes and aspirations for the future of the railways. It must have been a bitter disappointment to him, as to his audiences, that the subsequent destructive strikes and apparent incomprehension of what is required for survival jeopardised progress of the industry and the potential of his efforts within the time-scale of his service.

He has given freely of his time to talk to assemblies of retired staff and to individuals to keep them up-to-date – an aspect very much appreciated by those concerned. And within his busy complex job Sir Peter has shown a practical interest in the well-being of railway charities which play no small part in the senior citizens' league in his capacity as president of the Railway Convalescent Homes and the Railway Benevolent Institution. We wish him well.

★　★　★

Ronnie Ross, a former guard at Garston, advises any railway pensioner who feels down-hearted 'to put pen to paper and write their life and experiences on the railway'. Starting as a 'knocker-up' gave him scope for a story, which was published, and this was followed by others published or read on Radio Merseyside. Fraught with health problems Ronnie nevertheless has written four more stories which are now waiting publication.

★　★　★

A meeting of the BTSF in London reported that a strong resolution and comments about the report of the Serpell Committee, which had been sent to the Secretary of State for Transport, had brought a reply saying that the views of the Federation 'have been taken into account'. It was agreed to continue to use all available means to keep these views before the Government and the public. Among other items discussed was a communication from 'Pensioners of Peace' seeking sponsorship. This group supports unilateral disarmament which is outside the scope of the aims of the Federation.

★　★　★

A summer outing of Old Southeronians' Association Sussex No 1 Branch attracted 150 members who went on a cruise from Portsmouth harbour. The specially-chartered ship sailed over the Western Solent and up the Beaulieu River, with a stop for lunch at Bucklers Hard where many of Nelson's ships were built. The party visited the restored craftsmen's cottages and Maritime Museum finally landing at Clarence Pier, Southsea. Other social activities arranged for the 700 members of the branch include two 'get togethers' at Lancing, lunch at Hove Town Hall and a week's holiday at Falmouth.

NOVEMBER 1983

I BELIEVE the appointment of Bob Reid as chairman of British Rail will bring considerable satisfaction to many retired members of the railway community.

Those who have known him throughout his career have observed his qualities and dedication to the industry. His ability to identify what needs to be done to secure survival and make progress in the future make his appointment particularly welcome.

We offer him our congratulations.

★　★　★

A LETTER to Platform suggesting *Railnews* should not be available to other than 'staff and families of BR and subsidiary undertakings' prompts comment.

I do hope this correspondent is not suggesting withholding the newspaper from retired people, too. Many former employees wish to know what is happening on our railways. Yes – and how goes the image, warts and all!

But there is a real and positive reason for encouraging a wider audience to read the paper and learn more about the practical side of railway life. Look at the interest in the National Railway Museum, the profile publication and circulation of books and magazines on railway matters old and new, as well as the army of enthusiasts who give time, thought and effort to run the fascinating small railway companies throughout the country. Such zeal should be encouraged and directed with the same dedication as BR.

Rather than restrict the circulation of *Railnews* I believe it should be more widely available. About a million people visit the National Railway Museum every year. If Railnews was available to this captive public how much better informed existing or potential passengers would be, with almost certainly a stimulation of rail travel as a result.

The footnote to the letter in the August issue makes it clear that would-be readers not currently employed by BR may obtain copies of *Railnews* by sending a £3 annual subscription to cover postage and this course is recommended to retired staff who have no alternative access to copies.

DECEMBER 1983

WHAT'S it like to be retired? With the prospect of retirement at 55 instead of 65 or later many staff must be wondering what is in store for them. How are they, these youngsters, viewing the forced adjustment to their lives; what have they prepared; how will they use their time and what will they do apart from hammering the Super Fund?

It can be great fun! When you attend a meeting of retired staff notice how well and how young they all look. Sunburnt from travelling to those foreign parts, in working days so long out of reach; bright-eyed from sparring with the erstwhile boss; highly-critical of those who 'don't know how to run a railway' and bragging about new achievements in cookery, golf, gardening or tiddlywinks.

One thing is certain: if any aptitude for committee work is evident, be it in local government, politics, charity work or just a favourite society, the duties of committee membership, secretary or chairman will be showered on the unsuspecting and there will be no more spare time. 'How did I find time to go to work' will describe the situation while the voice from the kitchen will sing out 'which hat are you wearing today and when are you really going to retire?'

So if you are about to retire, be in good heart and let your colleagues now taking the flak know that they are contributing enough to keep the superannuation funds viable. For sooner than they think the time will arrive for the fun to start for them too!

APPENDIX C

The NER 'Mile by Mile'

Reproduced from *Mile by Mile on the LNER*
by S. N. Pike.

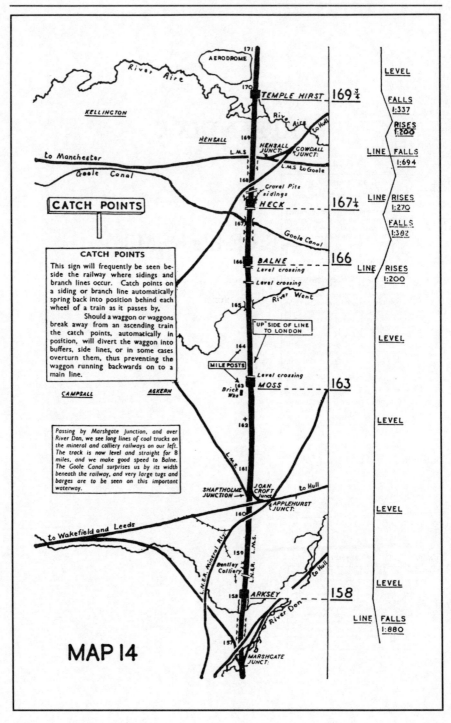

CATCH POINTS

CATCH POINTS

This sign will frequently be seen beside the railway where sidings and branch lines occur. Catch points on a siding or branch line automatically spring back into position behind each wheel of a train as it passes by,

Should a waggon or waggons break away from an ascending train the catch points, automatically in position, will divert the waggon into buffers, side lines, or in some cases overturn them, thus preventing the waggon running backwards on to a main line.

Passing by Marshgate Junction, and over River Don, we see long lines of coal trucks on the mineral and colliery railways on our left. The track is now level and straight for 8 miles, and we make good speed to Balne. The Goole Canal surprises us by its width beneath the railway, and very large tugs and barges are to be seen on this important waterway.

MAP 14

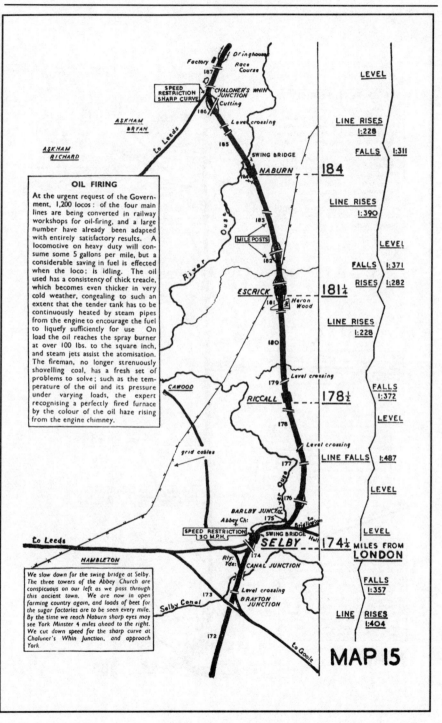

OIL FIRING

At the urgent request of the Government, 1,200 locos : of the four main lines are being converted in railway workshops for oil-firing, and a large number have already been adapted with entirely satisfactory results. A locomotive on heavy duty will consume some 5 gallons per mile, but a considerable saving in fuel is effected when the loco: is idling. The oil used has a consistency of thick treacle, which becomes even thicker in very cold weather, congealing to such an extent that the tender tank has to be continuously heated by steam pipes from the engine to encourage the fuel to liquefy sufficiently for use On load the oil reaches the spray burner at over 100 lbs. to the square inch, and steam jets assist the atomisation. The fireman, no longer strenuously shovelling coal, has a fresh set of problems to solve ; such as the temperature of the oil and its pressure under varying loads, the expert recognising a perfectly fired furnace by the colour of the oil haze rising from the engine chimney.

We slow down for the swing bridge at Selby. The three towers of the Abbey Church are conspicuous on our left as we pass through this ancient town. We are now in open farming country again, and loads of beet for the sugar factories are to be seen every mile. By the time we reach Naburn sharp eyes may see York Minster 4 miles ahead to the right. We cut down speed for the sharp curve at Chaloner's Whin Junction, and approach York.

MAP 15

LEVEL

LINE RISES 1:228

FALLS 1:311

184

LINE RISES 1:390

LEVEL

FALLS 1:371

RISES 1:282

181¼

LINE RISES 1:228

FALLS 1:372

178½

LEVEL

LINE FALLS 1:487

LEVEL

LEVEL

174½ MILES FROM LONDON

FALLS 1:357

LINE RISES 1:404

Factory

Dringhouses Race Course

187

SPEED RESTRICTION SHARP CURVE

CHALONER'S WHIN JUNCTION

Cutting

186

ASKHAM BRYAN

Level crossing

185

ASKHAM RICHARD

To Leeds

SWING BRIDGE

NABURN

184

River Ouse

183

MILE POSTS

182

ESCRICK

181

Heron Wood

180

CAWOOD

179

Level crossing

RICCALL

178

Level crossing

grid cables

177

River Ouse

176

BARLBY JUNCT.

Abbey Ch:

175

to Bridlington

to Hull

SPEED RESTRICTION 30 M.P.H.

SWING BRIDGE

SELBY

174

To Leeds

NAMBLETON

Rly: Yds:

CANAL JUNCTION

173

Level crossing

BRAYTON JUNCTION

Selby Canal

172

to Goole

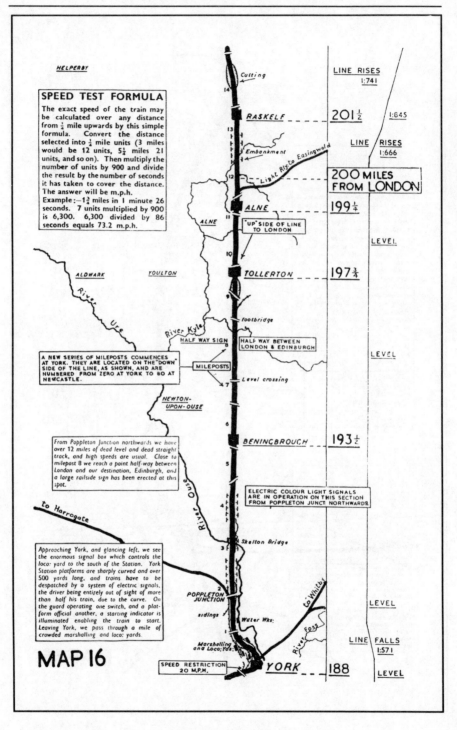

HELPERBY

SPEED TEST FORMULA

The exact speed of the train may be calculated over any distance from ¼ mile upwards by this simple formula. Convert the distance selected into ¼ mile units (3 miles would be 12 units, 5¼ miles 21 units, and so on). Then multiply the number of units by 900 and divide the result by the number of seconds it has taken to cover the distance. The answer will be m.p.h.

Example:—1¾ miles in 1 minute 26 seconds. 7 units multiplied by 900 is 6,300. 6,300 divided by 86 seconds equals 73.2 m.p.h.

Cutting

RASKELF

Embankment

Light Rly. to Easingwold

ALNE

"UP" SIDE OF LINE TO LONDON

TOLLERTON

footbridge

River Kyle

HALF WAY SIGN

HALF WAY BETWEEN LONDON & EDINBURGH

MILEPOSTS

Level crossing

LINE RISES 1:741

201½

1:645

LINE RISES 1:666

200 MILES FROM LONDON

199¼

LEVEL

197¾

LEVEL

ALDWARK

YOULTON

River Ure

ALNE

A NEW SERIES OF MILEPOSTS COMMENCES AT YORK. THEY ARE LOCATED ON THE "DOWN" SIDE OF THE LINE, AS SHOWN, AND ARE NUMBERED FROM ZERO AT YORK TO 80 AT NEWCASTLE.

NEWTON-UPON-OUSE

From Poppleton Junction northwards we have over 12 miles of dead level and dead straight track, and high speeds are usual. Close to milepost 8 we reach a point half-way between London and our destination, Edinburgh, and a large railside sign has been erected at this spot.

BENINGBROUGH

193½

ELECTRIC COLOUR LIGHT SIGNALS ARE IN OPERATION ON THIS SECTION FROM POPPLETON JUNCT. NORTHWARDS

LEVEL

River Ouse

to Harrogate

Skelton Bridge

Approaching York, and glancing left, we see the enormous signal box which controls the loco: yard to the south of the Station. York Station platforms are sharply curved and over 500 yards long, and trains have to be despatched by a system of electric signals, the driver being entirely out of sight of more than half his train, due to the curve. On the guard operating one switch, and a platform official another, a starting indicator is illuminated enabling the train to start. Leaving York, we pass through a mile of crowded marshalling and loco: yards.

POPPLETON JUNCTION

sidings

to Whitby

River Foss

Water Wks:

LEVEL

LINE FALLS 1:571

MAP 16

Marshalling and Loco: Yds:

SPEED RESTRICTION 20 M.P.H.

YORK

188

LEVEL

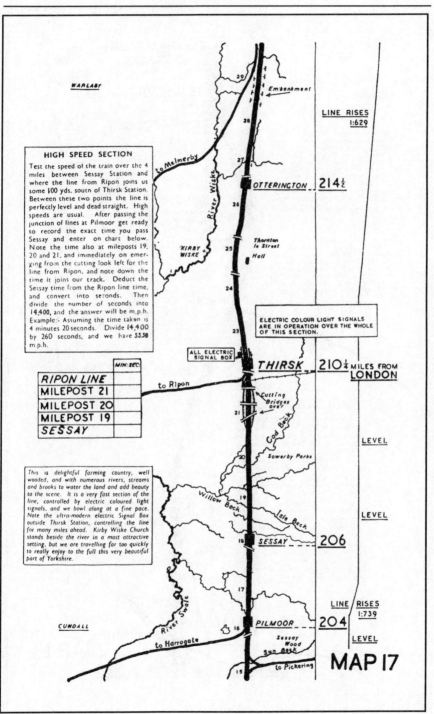

WARLABY

Embankment

LINE RISES
1:629

HIGH SPEED SECTION

Test the speed of the train over the 4 miles between Sessay Station and where the line from Ripon joins us some 100 yds. south of Thirsk Station. Between these two points the line is perfectly level and dead straight. High speeds are usual. After passing the junction of lines at Pilmoor get ready to record the exact time you pass Sessay and enter on chart below. Note the time also at mileposts 19, 20 and 21, and immediately on emerging from the cutting look left for the line from Ripon, and note down the time it joins our track. Deduct the Sessay time from the Ripon line time, and convert into seconds. Then divide the number of seconds into 14,400, and the answer will be m.p.h. Example:- Assuming the time taken is 4 minutes 20 seconds. Divide 14,400 by 260 seconds, and we have 55.38 m.p.h.

to Melmerby

River Wiske

OTTERINGTON 214½

Thornton le Street Hall

KIRBY WISKE

ELECTRIC COLOUR LIGHT SIGNALS ARE IN OPERATION OVER THE WHOLE OF THIS SECTION.

ALL ELECTRIC SIGNAL BOX

THIRSK 210¼ MILES FROM **LONDON**

to Ripon

Cutting Bridges over

	MIN: SEC.
RIPON LINE	
MILEPOST 21	
MILEPOST 20	
MILEPOST 19	
SESSAY	

Cod Beck

LEVEL

Sowerby Parks

This is delightful farming country, well wooded, and with numerous rivers, streams and brooks to water the land and add beauty to the scene. It is a very fast section of the line, controlled by electric coloured light signals, and we bowl along at a fine pace. Note the ultra-modern electric Signal Box outside Thirsk Station, controlling the line for many miles ahead. Kirby Wiske Church stands beside the river in a most attractive setting, but we are travelling far too quickly to really enjoy to the full this very beautiful part of Yorkshire.

Willow Beck

Isle Beck

LEVEL

SESSAY 206

CUNDALL

River Swale

to Harrogate

17

LINE RISES 1:739

PILMOOR 204

Sessay Wood gun Beck

LEVEL

to Pickering

MAP 17

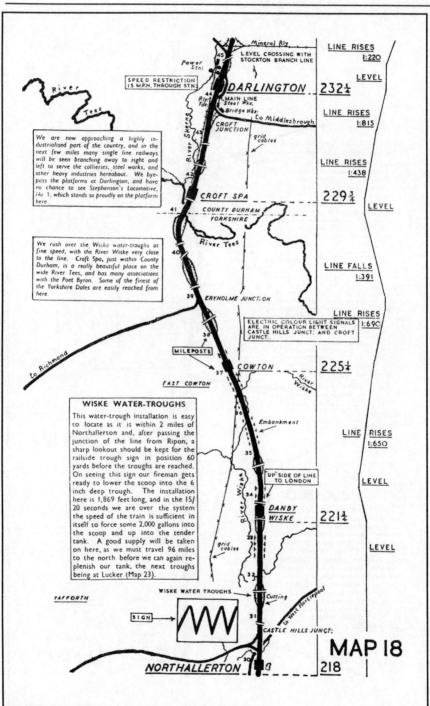

LINE RISES 1:220

Mineral Rly
LEVEL CROSSING WITH
STOCKTON BRANCH LINE

Power Stn:

SPEED RESTRICTION
15 M.P.H. THROUGH STN.

DARLINGTON 232½ LEVEL

Rly Yds.

Main Line
Steel Wks.
Bridge Wks.

To Middlesbrough

LINE RISES 1:815

CROFT JUNCTION

River Skerne

grid cables

LINE RISES 1:438

We are now approaching a highly in-
dustrialised part of the country, and in the
next few miles many single line railways
will be seen branching away to right and
left to serve the collieries, steel works, and
other heavy industries hereabout. We bye-
pass the platforms at Darlington, and have
no chance to see Stephenson's Locomotive,
No 1, which stands so proudly on the platform
here.

CROFT SPA 229¾ LEVEL

COUNTY DURHAM
YORKSHIRE

River Tees

We rush over the Wiske water-troughs at
fine speed, with the River Wiske very close
to the line. Croft Spa, just within County
Durham, is a really beautiful place on the
wide River Tees, and has many associations
with the Poet Byron. Some of the finest of
the Yorkshire Dales are easily reached from
here.

LINE FALLS 1:391

ERYHOLME JUNCTION

LINE RISES 1:690

ELECTRIC COLOUR LIGHT SIGNALS
ARE IN OPERATION BETWEEN
CASTLE HILLS JUNCT. AND CROFT
JUNCT.

to Richmond

MILEPOSTS

COWTON 225¼

River Wiske

EAST COWTON

WISKE WATER-TROUGHS

This water-trough installation is easy
to locate as it is within 2 miles of
Northallerton and, after passing the
junction of the line from Ripon, a
sharp lookout should be kept for the
railside trough sign in position 60
yards before the troughs are reached.
On seeing this sign our fireman gets
ready to lower the scoop into the 6
inch deep trough. The installation
here is 1,869 feet long, and in the 15/
20 seconds we are over the system
the speed of the train is sufficient in
itself to force some 2,000 gallons into
the scoop and up into the tender
tank. A good supply will be taken
on here, as we must travel 96 miles
to the north before we can again re-
plenish our tank, the next troughs
being at Lucker (Map 23).

Embankment

LINE RISES 1:650

LEVEL

"UP" SIDE OF LINE
TO LONDON

River Wiske

**DANBY
WISKE** 221¼

grid cables

LEVEL

YAFFORTH

WISKE WATER TROUGHS

Cutting

SIGN

to West Hartlepool

CASTLE HILLS JUNCT.

MAP 18

218

NORTHALLERTON

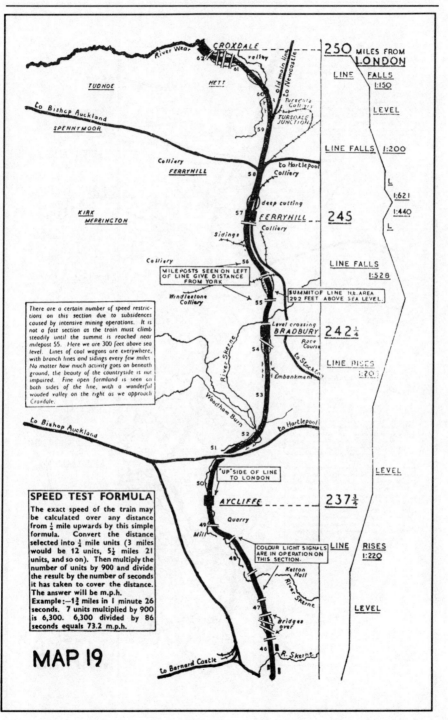

CROXDALE valley

250 MILES FROM **LONDON**

LINE FALLS 1:150

LEVEL

TUDHOE
HETT

To Bishop Auckland
SPENNYMOOR

LINE FALLS 1:200

L 1:621
1:440
L

Colliery
FERRYHILL

to Hartlepool
Colliery

deep cutting

KIRK MERRINGTON

FERRYHILL Colliery

245

Sidings

Colliery

MILEPOSTS SEEN ON LEFT
OF LINE GIVE DISTANCE
FROM YORK

LINE FALLS 1:528

Windlestone Colliery

SUMMIT OF LINE N.E. AREA
292 FEET ABOVE SEA LEVEL

There are a certain number of speed restrictions on this section due to subsidences
caused by intensive mining operations. It is
not a fast section as the train must climb
steadily until the summit is reached near
milepost 55. Here we are 300 feet above sea
level. Lines of coal wagons are everywhere,
with branch lines and sidings every few miles.
No matter how much activity goes on beneath
ground, the beauty of the countryside is not
impaired. Fine open farmland is seen on
both sides of the line, with a wonderful
wooded valley on the right as we approach
Croxdale.

Level crossing
BRADBURY

242¼

Race Course

to Stockton

River Skerne

LINE RISES 1:70

Embankment

To Bishop Auckland

Woodham Burn

to Hartlepool

"UP" SIDE OF LINE
TO LONDON

LEVEL

SPEED TEST FORMULA

The exact speed of the train may
be calculated over any distance
from ¼ mile upwards by this simple
formula. Convert the distance
selected into ¼ mile units (3 miles
would be 12 units, 5¼ miles 21
units, and so on). Then multiply the
number of units by 900 and divide
the result by the number of seconds
it has taken to cover the distance.
The answer will be m.p.h.
Example:—1¾ miles in 1 minute 26
seconds. 7 units multiplied by 900
is 6,300. 6,300 divided by 86
seconds equals 73.2 m.p.h.

AYCLIFFE

237¾

Quarry

Mill

COLOUR LIGHT SIGNALS
ARE IN OPERATION ON
THIS SECTION.

LINE RISES 1:220

Ketton Hall

River Skerne

LEVEL

Bridges over

MAP 19

to Barnard Castle

R. Skerne

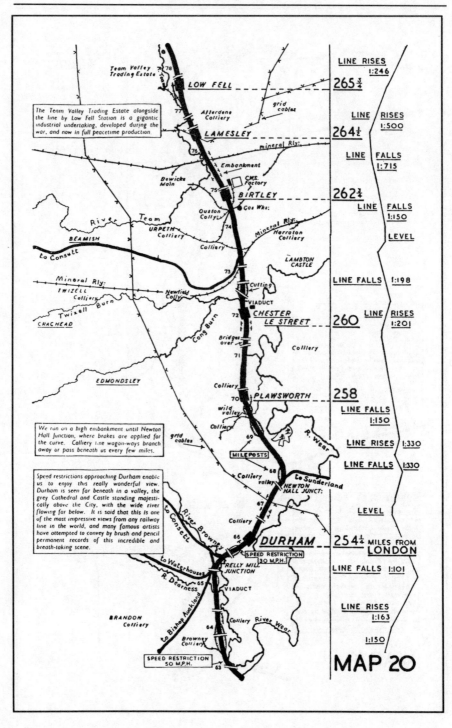

The Team Valley Trading Estate alongside the line by Low Fell Station is a gigantic industrial undertaking, developed during the war, and now in full peacetime production.

We run on a high embankment until Newton Hall Junction, where brakes are applied for the curve. Colliery line wagon-ways branch away or pass beneath us every few miles.

Speed restrictions approaching Durham enable us to enjoy this really wonderful view. Durham is seen far beneath in a valley, the grey Cathedral and Castle standing majestically above the City, with the wide river flowing far below. It is said that this is one of the most impressive views from any railway line in the world, and many famous artists have attempted to convey by brush and pencil permanent records of this incredible and breath-taking scene.

MAP 20

152

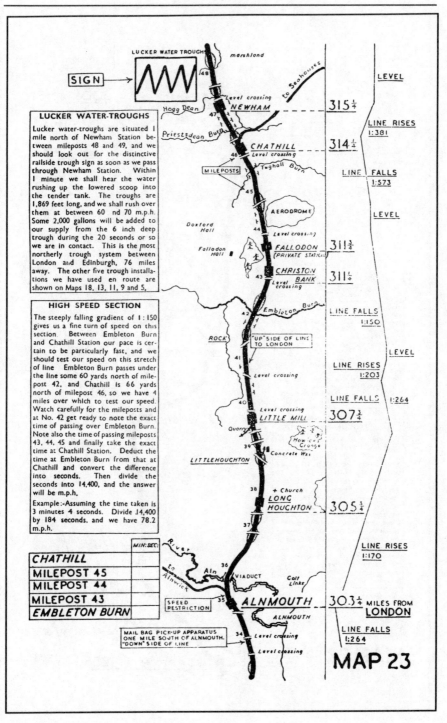

LUCKER WATER TROUGHS

SIGN →

marshland

To Seahouses

LEVEL

LUCKER WATER-TROUGHS

Lucker water-troughs are situated 1 mile north of Newham Station between mileposts 48 and 49, and we should look out for the distinctive railside trough sign as soon as we pass through Newham Station. Within 1 minute we shall hear the water rushing up the lowered scoop into the tender tank. The troughs are 1,869 feet long, and we shall rush over them at between 60 and 70 m.p.h. Some 2,000 gallons will be added to our supply from the 6 inch deep trough during the 20 seconds or so we are in contact. This is the most northerly trough system between London and Edinburgh, 76 miles away. The other five trough installations we have used en route are shown on Maps 18, 13, 11, 9 and 5.

Hogg Dean

Level crossing

NEWHAM

47

Priestedean Burn

46

CHATHILL
Level crossing

MILEPOSTS

Tughall Burn

45

AERODROME

Doxford Hall

44

Level crossing

Fallodon Hall

FALLODON
(PRIVATE STATION)

43

CHRISTON BANK
Level crossing

315¼

314¼

311¾

311¼

LINE RISES 1:381

LINE FALLS 1:573

LEVEL

HIGH SPEED SECTION

The steeply falling gradient of 1:150 gives us a fine turn of speed on this section. Between Embleton Burn and Chathill Station our pace is certain to be particularly fast, and we should test our speed on this stretch of line. Embleton Burn passes under the line some 60 yards north of milepost 42, and Chathill is 66 yards north of milepost 46, so we have 4 miles over which to test our speed. Watch carefully for the mileposts and at No. 42 get ready to note the exact time of passing over Embleton Burn. Note also the time of passing mileposts 43, 44, 45 and finally take the exact time at Chathill Station. Deduct the time at Embleton Burn from that at Chathill and convert the difference into seconds. Then divide the seconds into 14,400, and the answer will be m.p.h.

Example:- Assuming the time taken is 3 minutes 4 seconds. Divide 14,400 by 184 seconds, and we have 78.2 m.p.h.

42

Embleton Burn

ROCK

"UP" SIDE OF LINE TO LONDON

41

Level crossing

40

Level crossing

LITTLE MILL

Quarry

39

Howick Grange
Concrete Wks

LITTLEHOUGHTON

38

+ Church
LONG HOUGHTON

37

LINE FALLS 1:150

LEVEL

LINE RISES 1:203

LINE FALLS 1:264

307¾

305½

	MIN: SEC:
CHATHILL	
MILEPOST 45	
MILEPOST 44	
MILEPOST 43	
EMBLETON BURN	

River
Aln
to Alnwick

36

VIADUCT

Golf Links

35

SPEED RESTRICTION

ALNMOUTH

ALNMOUTH

LINE RISES 1:170

303¾ MILES FROM **LONDON**

LINE FALLS 1:264

MAIL BAG PICK-UP APPARATUS ONE MILE SOUTH OF ALNMOUTH. "DOWN" SIDE OF LINE

34

Level crossing

Level crossing

MAP 23

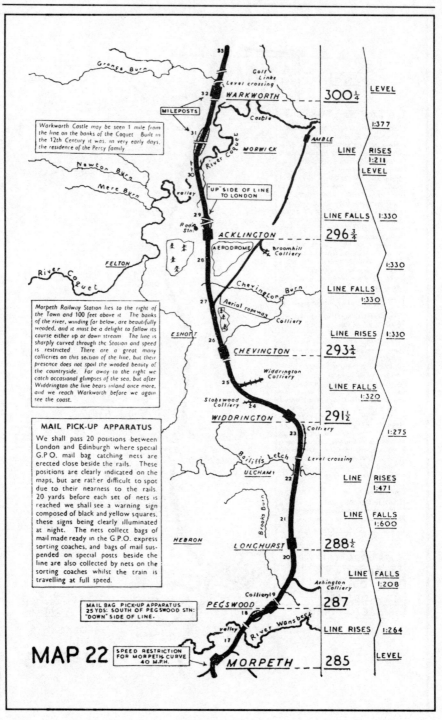

Warkworth Castle may be seen 1 mile from the line on the banks of the Coquet. Built in the 12th Century it was, in very early days, the residence of the Percy family.

MILEPOSTS

"UP" SIDE OF LINE TO LONDON

Morpeth Railway Station lies to the right of the Town and 100 feet above it. The banks of the river, winding far below, are beautifully wooded, and it must be a delight to follow its course either up or down stream. The line is sharply curved through the Station and speed is restricted. There are a great many collieries on this section of the line, but their presence does not spoil the wooded beauty of the countryside. Far away to the right we catch occasional glimpses of the sea, but after Widdrington the line bears inland once more, and we reach Warkworth before we again see the coast.

MAIL PICK-UP APPARATUS

We shall pass 20 positions between London and Edinburgh where special G.P.O. mail bag catching nets are erected close beside the rails. These positions are clearly indicated on the maps, but are rather difficult to spot due to their nearness to the rails. 20 yards before each set of nets is reached we shall see a warning sign composed of black and yellow squares, these signs being clearly illuminated at night. The nets collect bags of mail made ready in the G.P.O. express sorting coaches, and bags of mail suspended on special posts beside the line are also collected by nets on the sorting coaches whilst the train is travelling at full speed.

MAIL BAG PICK-UP APPARATUS
25 YDS: SOUTH OF PEGSWOOD STN:
"DOWN" SIDE OF LINE.

MAP 22

SPEED RESTRICTION FOR MORPETH CURVE 40 M.P.H.

WARKWORTH — 300¼ — LEVEL — 1:377

LINE RISES 1:211 — LEVEL

ACKLINGTON — 296¾ — LINE FALLS 1:330 — 1:330

LINE FALLS 1:330

CHEVINGTON — 293¼ — LINE RISES 1:330

WIDDRINGTON — 291½ — LINE FALLS 1:320 — 1:275

LINE RISES 1:471

LINE FALLS 1:600

LONGHURST — 288½

LINE FALLS 1:208

PEGSWOOD — 287

LINE RISES 1:264

MORPETH — 285 — LEVEL

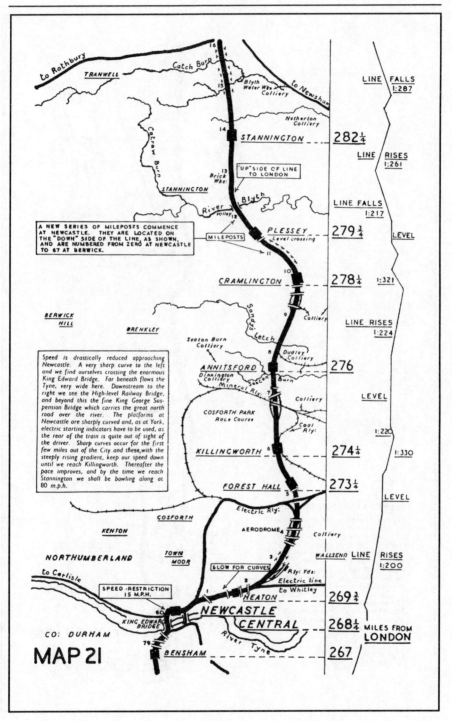

to Rothbury

TRANWELL

Catch Burn

Catlaw Burn

15

16

Blyth
Water Wks
Colliery

to Newsham

LINE FALLS
1:287

14

STANNINGTON

Netherton
Colliery

282¼

LINE RISES
1:261

13

Brick
Wks

"UP" SIDE OF LINE
TO LONDON

LINE FALLS
1:217

STANNINGTON

River   Blyth

Valley
12

MILEPOSTS

A NEW SERIES OF MILEPOSTS COMMENCE
AT NEWCASTLE. THEY ARE LOCATED ON
THE "DOWN" SIDE OF THE LINE, AS SHOWN,
AND ARE NUMBERED FROM ZERO AT NEWCASTLE
TO 67 AT BERWICK.

PLESSEY
Level crossing

279¾

LEVEL

11

CRAMLINGTON

10

278¼

1:321

9

Colliery

BERWICK
HILL

Sandys
Letch

LINE RISES
1:224

BRENKLEY

Seaton Burn
Colliery

8   Dudley
Colliery

Speed is drastically reduced approaching
Newcastle. A very sharp curve to the left
and we find ourselves crossing the enormous
King Edward Bridge. Far beneath flows the
Tyne, very wide here. Downstream to the
right we see the High-level Railway Bridge,
and beyond this the fine King George Sus-
pension Bridge which carries the great north
road over the river. The platforms at
Newcastle are sharply curved and, as at York,
electric starting indicators have to be used, as
the rear of the train is quite out of sight of
the driver. Sharp curves occur for the first
few miles out of the City and these, with the
steeply rising gradient, keep our speed down
until we reach Killingworth. Thereafter the
pace improves, and by the time we reach
Stannington we shall be bowling along at
80 m.p.h.

ANNITSFORD
Dinnington
Colliery

Seaton   Burn
Mineral Rly.
7

276

Colliery

LEVEL

COSFORTH PARK
Race Course

Coal
Rly:

1:220

KILLINGWORTH   6

274¼

1:330

FOREST HALL

5

273¼

LEVEL

COSFORTH

Electric Rly:

KENTON

TOWN
MOOR

AERODROME   4

Colliery

NORTHUMBERLAND

to Carlisle

SLOW FOR CURVES

3

WALLSEND   LINE RISES
1:200

Rly: Yds:
Electric line
to Whitley

SPEED RESTRICTION
15 M.P.H.

2

1

HEATON

269¾

80

KING EDWARD
BRIDGE

NEWCASTLE
CENTRAL

268¼

MILES FROM
LONDON

CO: DURHAM

MAP 21

79

BENSHAM

River Tyne

267

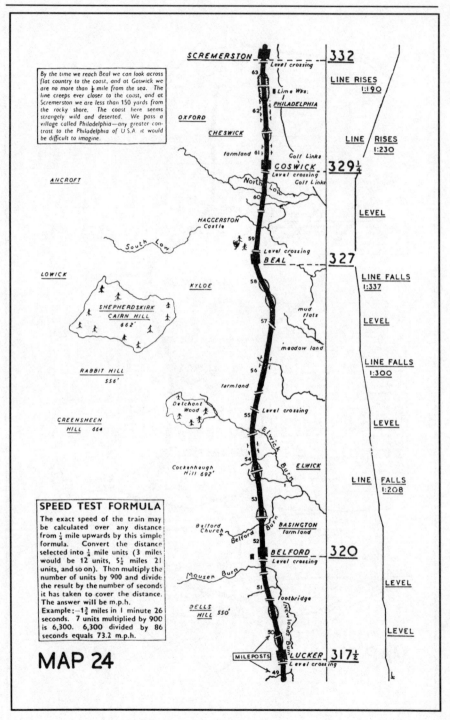

By the time we reach Beal we can look across flat country to the coast, and at Goswick we are no more than ½ mile from the sea. The line creeps ever closer to the coast, and at Scremerston we are less than 150 yards from the rocky shore. The coast here seems strangely wild and deserted. We pass a village called Philadelphia—any greater contrast to the Philadelphia of U.S.A. it would be difficult to imagine.

SCREMERSTON — 332
Level crossing
63
LINE RISES 1:190
Lime Whs:
62 **PHILADELPHIA**
OXFORD
CHESWICK
farmland 61 LINE RISES 1:230
Golf Links
GOSWICK — 329¼
Level crossing
Golf Links
ANCROFT North Low
60
HAGGERSTON Castle
LEVEL
59
Level crossing
BEAL — 327
LOWICK KYLOE
58 LINE FALLS 1:337
mud flats
SHEPHERDSKIRK CAIRN HILL 662'
57 LEVEL
meadow land
RABBIT HILL 556'
56 LINE FALLS 1:300
farmland
GREENSHEEN HILL 664
Dełchant Wood
55 LEVEL
Level crossing
Elwick Burn
54 **ELWICK**
Cockenheugh Hill 692'
53 LINE FALLS 1:208
Belford Church
BASINGTON farmland
52 Belford Burn
BELFORD — 320
Level crossing
Mousen Burn
51 LEVEL
footbridge
DELLS HILL 550'
New Swin Burn
LEVEL
50
MILEPOSTS **LUCKER** — 317½
Level crossing
49

SPEED TEST FORMULA
The exact speed of the train may be calculated over any distance from ¼ mile upwards by this simple formula. Convert the distance selected into ¼ mile units (3 miles would be 12 units, 5¼ miles 21 units, and so on). Then multiply the number of units by 900 and divide the result by the number of seconds it has taken to cover the distance. The answer will be m.p.h.
Example:—1¾ miles in 1 minute 26 seconds. 7 units multiplied by 900 is 6,300. 6,300 divided by 86 seconds equals 73.2 m.p.h.

MAP 24

156

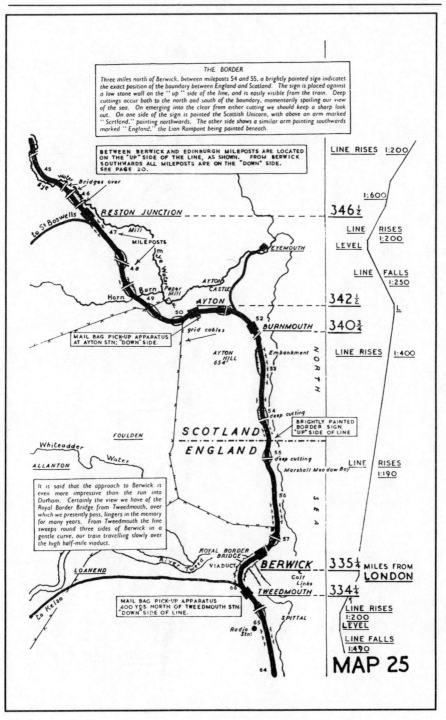

THE BORDER

Three miles north of Berwick, between mileposts 54 and 55, a brightly painted sign indicates the exact position of the boundary between England and Scotland. The sign is placed against a low stone wall on the "up" side of the line, and is easily visible from the train. Deep cuttings occur both to the north and south of the boundary, momentarily spoiling our view of the sea. On emerging into the clear from either cutting we should keep a sharp look out. On one side of the sign is painted the Scottish Unicorn, with above an arm marked "Scotland," pointing northwards. The other side shows a similar arm pointing southwards marked "England," the Lion Rampant being painted beneath.

BETWEEN BERWICK AND EDINBURGH MILEPOSTS ARE LOCATED ON THE "UP" SIDE OF THE LINE, AS SHOWN. FROM BERWICK SOUTHWARDS ALL MILEPOSTS ARE ON THE "DOWN" SIDE. SEE PAGE 20.

LINE RISES 1:200

1:600

RESTON JUNCTION — 346½

LINE RISES 1:200

LINE LEVEL

LINE FALLS 1:250

342½

340¾ — BURNMOUTH

LINE RISES 1:400

MAIL BAG PICK-UP APPARATUS AT AYTON STN; "DOWN" SIDE.

BRIGHTLY PAINTED BORDER SIGN, "UP" SIDE OF LINE

SCOTLAND
ENGLAND

LINE RISES 1:190

It is said that the approach to Berwick is even more impressive than the run into Durham. Certainly the view we have of the Royal Border Bridge from Tweedmouth, over which we presently pass, lingers in the memory for many years. From Tweedmouth the line sweeps round three sides of Berwick in a gentle curve, our train travelling slowly over the high half-mile viaduct.

ROYAL BORDER BRIDGE
VIADUCT

BERWICK — 335¼ MILES FROM LONDON

TWEEDMOUTH — 334¼

MAIL BAG PICK-UP APPARATUS 400 YDS. NORTH OF TWEEDMOUTH STN; "DOWN" SIDE OF LINE.

LINE RISES 1:200
LEVEL
LINE FALLS 1:490

MAP 25

INDEX